County Companion

To Dad

Happy Birthday 1985
Love
from
Merv

Surrey

Hilary Arnold

GW00601277

Cadogan Books London

CONTENTS

Illustrations: Pauline Pears
Series design by Information Design Workshop
Cartography: Line and Line
Editors: Leone Turner
        Kate Raison

© Cadogan Books Ltd 1984
ISBN 0 946313 25 3

First published in 1984 by Cadogan Books Ltd, 16 Lower Marsh, London SE1 7RJ in association with Century Publishing Co. Ltd, Portland House, 12–13 Greek Street, London W1V 5IE
Reprinted 1985 by
Cadogan Books Ltd

Typeset in Great Britain by Felbrook, Penge, London
Printed in Great Britain by Purnell & Sons Ltd, Paulton, Bristol

Leisure A-Z   **120**

Acknowledgements

How to use this guide

Complete Guide

The first section of the book describes all the major towns and villages of interest in Surrey. They are included, along with outstanding attractions, in alphabetical order. After each name there is a map reference locating the place on one of the detailed maps. Places of interest to be found in the various towns and villages are described in this section but all details of their opening times, charges, facilities and other information can be found in the Leisure Directory. All places of interest in bold have a listing in the Leisure Directory under the relevant section. For example:

Hampton Court Palace
(Historic Homes)
This indicates that details for Hampton Court Palace can be found in the Historic Homes section of the Leisure Directory.
Farnham Museum indicates that details for this museum can be found under the Museums section of the Leisure Directory.

Maps

A full map of Surrey showing all major roads can be found on pages 108 & 109. This is followed by four detailed maps of sections of Surrey on which are located all major places of interest and other important features such as caravan parks.

Town Directory

The major towns are listed here with the facilities and places of interest to be found in and nearby those towns. All details about the places to visit can be found in the Leisure Directory. For example:
Museum: Brooking Collection
This indicates that details for the Brooking Collection (under Guildford in the Town Directory) can be found in the Museums section of the Leisure Directory.
   Street Plans of some major towns can also be found in this section with places of interest located.

Leisure A-Z

This section lists activities and places to visit, giving all important details. A full list of the topics included can be found on the Contents list at the front of this book. All entries are in alphabetical order. Where relevant, a map reference is given immediately after the name of the place of interest, locating it on one of the detailed maps. A page reference is given if the place is described in the Complete Guide.

The telephone number of the place is then given, followed by the location and all other details.

Symbols

🚐 caravan park
🎣 angling
⛳₁₈ golf course
ℹ️ tourist information centre
🅿️ Parking
🍴 licensed restaurant
🛋️ snacks
♿ access for disabled visitors
🛍️ shop
🎡 picnic site
🏊 swimming pool
🍷 bar
⛵ sailing
∪ riding
⛺ campsite
PO post office
▼ place of interest

DofE Standard Opening Times

The following opening hours apply to all buildings and other historic monuments which are managed by the Department of the Environment. Some buildings and monuments are open for further periods in the summer and these extra opening hours are listed with the entry in the Leisure Directory.

March-April & October:
Weekdays 9.30-17.30
Sundays 14.00-17.30
May-September:
Weekdays 9.30-19.00
Sundays 14.00-19.00
November-February:
Weekdays 9.30-16.00
Sundays 14.00-16.00

All DofE buildings and monuments are closed on December 24-26 and January 1. Some of them also close for the lunch hour which is normally 13.00-14.00

Complete Guide

Abinger Map 2 Ac

Abinger Hammer is one of Surrey's best-known
villages. It was established in medieval times as a
centre for the local iron industry, hence the
'Hammer' in its name. The old hammer ponds
which served that industry are now planted with
watercress and fed with fresh spring water rather
than water from the Tillingbourne river as they once
were. The river is narrow here, contained within
brick walls. For centuries it turned the wheels of a
string of watermills, grinding gunpowder, corn, and
powering forges and looms.

This pretty village lies in some of the most
delightful wooded land in the county. There are
delightful tile-hung cottages in the centre, some very
old and others good replicas of the old style. Here,
too, is Abinger's famous landmark: a hammer clock.
It stands out from the corner of Clock House, built in
1891, suspended above the busy Guildford to Dorking
road. Every hour the bell is struck by 'Jack the
Smith', a reminder of the village's iron-forging days.
The clock is in memory of the 1st Lord Farrer.

About a mile from Abinger is one of the finest
buildings in the district, a seventeenth-century
farmhouse, Crossways Farm. There is a fifteenth-
century farmhouse just east of the village called
Paddington Farm. Two other famous farms lie in
Sutton, to the west, namely **Sutton Place Farm**
(Gardens), built about 1700, and Fulvens Farm,
dating from the mid-seventeenth century.

The church of St James dates back to the twelfth
century, but was virtually destroyed by a bomb
during the Second World War. It was well restored
in 1950 and again in 1964. In the churchyard is a
war memorial designed by the architect Edwin
Lutyens.

Lutyens was designing buildings during the end of
the nineteenth and the early part of this century. He

is particularly renowned in Surrey, for it was here that he carried out so much of his highly-regarded work, both in restoring and extending old buildings without spoiling their original style, and in planning new edifices. One of his first patrons was Gertrude Jekyll, the artist and historian, who lived for much of her life in Surrey. She is famous for her garden designs, many of which provide a perfect setting for Lutyens houses. One example of this is Goddards, built by Lutyens in 1898 and featuring a Gertrude Jekyll garden.

Goddards was once the home of Sidney Webb, one of many intellectuals attracted to Abinger. E.M. Forster lived in Abinger Hammer from 1902-1945 and the village forms the central theme for a collection of his essays, *Abinger Harvest*, published in 1936. Max Beerbohm, the writer and cartoonist, lived in Abinger Manor Cottage, in the village

The bell at Abinger Common

A

centre, during the Second World War.

The parish of Abinger is the longest in Surrey, stretching for nine-and-a-half miles and taking in, not only Abinger Hammer, but another village, Abinger Common. Goddards is in Abinger Common, a village without a real centre but set in some of the loveliest scenery in the southeast. The area has fine woodland and commands far-reaching views from its high elevation on the edge of the Surrey Hills, part of the North Downs. In June the hamlet stages a **Medieval Fair** (Events) in which the entire village sports colourful dress.

Addington Map 3 Bc

Addington is no longer strictly in Surrey but part of Greater London, like other sections of the old county which border the metropolis. Less than 12 miles from Charing Cross, in a valley near Croydon, it is a simple village, with old brick cottages, and has a long history. The old manor estate here was Addington Park which dates back to Saxon times and was mentioned in the Domesday Book. After the Norman Conquest it is reputed to have been given by King William to his cook, Tezelin. For centuries the manor was the home of the Leigh family, three generations of whom are commemorated in the village's Norman church. One of their memorials is a lovely Tudor brass to John Leigh who died in 1509. St Mary's has many other fine memorials. Thomas Hatteclyff, who died in 1540 and was Henry VIII's Master of the Household, commands a brass on the chancel floor. There is a delightful monument to Sir Olliphe Leigh surrounded by his family and ancestors and created on his death in 1612. The Trecothick family with their unusual names is remembered in various generations. Mrs Grizzel Trecothick has a fine monument for her death in

1769, as does Barlow Trecothick who died in 1775 and was once Lord Mayor of London.

Five Archbishops of Canterbury are buried in the church. They had a palace here in the nineteenth century, Addington Palace. The lovely house was first built for Barlow Trecothick in the 1770s and now houses the Royal School for Church Music.

Albury Map 2 Ac

The present village of Albury has existed only since the mid-nineteenth century. Before then it was a small settlement called Weston Street and Albury village was connected to its old manor half a mile to the east. As a result this is a rather contrived though extremely attractive village in a lovely situation on the Tillingbourne Valley.

The local manor was **Albury Park** (Historic Homes). Originally a Tudor Mansion, the Duke of Norfolk had it rebuilt in the seventeenth century and John Evelyn laid out the lovely gardens to complement the new-style house. When William Cobbett passed through the district in 1822 he described the gardens as 'the prettiest that I ever saw in England'. The house underwent several further alterations over the years and in 1846-52 it was completely restyled to a mock-Tudor design by the architect A.W.N. Pugin. The chimneys which resulted are extraordinary. There are 63 of them, all highly ornate and in various Tudor styles.

For much of the nineteenth century, Albury Park was owned by a wealthy banker and politician, Henry Drummond, who acquired the house in 1819. Drummond not only restyled his house and encouraged the removal of the village to Weston Street, but also made his home a centre for the Catholic Apostolic Church. Edward Irving founded the church, creating a storm in London when he

A

packed his chapel in Hatton Garden with people eager to hear his new preaching. Both his style as an orator and his ritualistic method of worship were unorthodox to the extent that Irving was eventually tried for heresy. Though the case against him failed, he lost many supporters. Henry Drummond continued as one of Irving's most enthusiastic supporters and in 1840 he built a church for him which stands north of Albury Park.

Albury's original parish church is nearby in the grounds of Albury Park, where the village once stood. Since it was abandoned by the villagers in 1842 it has avoided excessive restoration and remains a particularly attractive ancient building. There are still sections of the Saxon original and outstanding Norman features including the tower. William Oughtred, an influential mathematician who numbered amongst his contributions the invention of the multiplication sign, was rector at the church from 1610-1660. He died at Albury but the place of his burial is not known. Henry Drummond was buried in the lovely old church within a thirteenth-century chapel.

Drummond built another church for the new village. St Peter and St Paul Church was built in 1842. Drummond had hoped for a Romanesque-style building in stone but he was away during the construction and it was carried out in brick.

South of the village at Farley Heath are the remains of an important Roman settlement, said to have been one of the largest in Britain. Amongst them are the ruins of a temple which is believed to have been destroyed in the fifth century. A wealth of Roman coins and other finds have been discovered there. The site was first excavated by Martin Tupper, a well-known 'philosopher' and writer, in 1848. In his story 'Stephen Langton' he wrote about a deep, sparkling pond which lies nearby, the Silent Pool.

Blackheath, on the hills above Albury, is a Victorian hamlet. It stands beside an extensive common and in the pine woods nearby is a Franciscan monastery built in 1895.

Alfold Map 2 Bc

In the south of the village stands a fine old church which, with the two tile-hung cottages standing by it, represents a delightful Surrey scene. St Nicholas church dates from Norman times and is a typical Wealden church of the period. Inside is a rare and ancient twelfth-century font. The church porches are fourteenth century and approached along a delightful paved path beside the old cottages whose tiles are hung in scalloped patterns.

The village was established as a centre for glassmaking from the middle ages. The industry was revitalized in the sixteenth century when glassmakers from Lorraine, led by Jean Le Carré who is buried in the churchyard, settled here. This is an area of lovely woodland even today and it was from this local timber that charcoal was once made for the process of making Alfold glass.

Ashtead Map 3 Ba

The old settlement lies on a major road between Epsom and Leatherhead. Inevitably, as these towns grew into virtual London suburbs, old Ashtead was incorporated into the development yet it still retains an identity of its own. The Romans were early settlers on Ashtead Common where the excavation of Roman remains in the 1920s revealed an extensive villa. Ancient earthworks can be seen closeby the church of St Giles which also contain Roman materials. It is believed that some of the Roman tiles here originally came from the villa on Ashtead Common where there is evidence of a tile factory. St

B

Giles itself dates from the sixteenth century when an older church was rebuilt. It was again restored in the second half of the nineteenth century. One of the stained-glass windows, depicting the crucifixion, is sixteenth century and originates from a Flemish monastery. There are also several notable monuments, including one to Diana Fielding which is attributed to the great eighteenth-century monument sculptor J.M. Rysbrack and dated 1733. Another famous craftsman, Grinling Gibbons the master woodcarver, is said to have modelled the monument to Henry Newdigate who died in 1629, though it is not in his usual fine and elaborate style.

Ashtead Park is the grand house of the district, built in 1790 to a design by Joseph Bonomi but carried out by Samuel Wyatt. The sturdy brick building now houses the City of London Freemen's school.

Bagshot Map 1 Bb

Situated close to Camberley and Aldershot, Bagshot has become a satellite of these army towns and flourishes as a result. The town does not contain any outstanding architecture but the area is justly known for its splendid flowering shrubs, with rhododendrons and azaleas providing a magnificent display of colour in early summer. Holly also grows profusely in the area.

In the past this was an important staging post for journeys west of London. Bagshot Heath was notoriously dangerous for travellers, with highwaymen and brigands taking full advantage of its barren loneliness. Daniel Defoe wrote a much-quoted description of the heath in 1724: '...here is a vast tract of land, some of it within seventeen or eighteen miles of the capital city, which is not only poor but even quite sterile, given up for barrenness, horrid and frightful to look upon, not only good for little, but good for nothing; much of it is sandy desert, and one may frequently be put in mind of Arabia Deserta...'. Today parts of this eerie expanse are used for army manoeuvres, so it remains uninviting. The area was also a hunting ground for monarchs and Bagshot Park, now used as a training centre by the army, was originally a hunting lodge for James I and Charles I. The present building, a mock-Tudor brick house, was erected for Queen Victoria's son, the Duke of Connaught, in 1877. The Military Academy just south of Sandhurst houses **The Royal Military Academy Sandhurst Collection** (Museums).

Banstead Map 3 Bb

Situated close enough to London to be taken in by the suburban sprawl, Banstead nonetheless retains its own character. It has a fine old church, All Saints, dating from the late twelfth century.

Banstead Common and **Banstead Woods** (Woodland) provide delightful areas for walking. Banstead Woods was originally the estate of a large country house. The present building, an attractive design by Norman Shaw, dates from 1844 and has been greatly extended for use as a hospital. The woods are owned by Surrey County Council with easy access to over 300 acres of magificent trees heightened in spring by a carpet of bluebells and in early summer by flowering rhododendrons. Within this woodland is **Perrott Wood** (Nature Reserve), an open nature reserve where a wide range of birds can be seen and a nature trail can be explored.

Barnes Map 3 Bb

This delightful riverside settlement has now been incorporated into Greater London and provides one of

B

the capital's most attractive 'villages'. Standing on a broad bend of the Thames, its charming streets are lined with Georgian and Victorian cottages, many of them with weatherboarding, which give a true village atmosphere. As well as the lovely river front, there is also Barnes Common near the centre and a pretty green, complete with pond.

The village was named after the manor house, Barn Elms, home of Queen Elizabeth I's Secretary of State, Sir Francis Walsingham, from 1579-1590. It was later the home of the Earl of Essex, another of Elizabeth's favourites, and the house is frequently mentioned in Samuel Pepys' diary as a place of public entertainment. Later the estate was used in part by one of the most exclusive sports clubs in the world, the Ranelagh Club, founded in 1884 and known for its polo, tennis and golf activities. However, the old manor was destroyed in 1954 and the playing fields of the rich became playing fields for the locals.

Other famous people who have lived in Barnes include Sir Philip Sidney who married Walsingham's daughter and lived at Barn Elms. Henry Fielding, author of *Tom Jones*, lived in Milburne House overlooking the village green from 1748-53. William Cobbett, the political writer, rented a house on the Barn Elms estate from 1828-30 where he wrote his *Advice to Young Men* and edited his *Weekly Political Register*.

Perhaps Barnes' most appreciated buildings is the delightful row of houses, Barnes Terrace, which faces the river. They are eighteenth century with wrought-iron verandas and balconies providing their owners with an exterior position from which to view the Thames. Among Barnes' other outstanding buildings is a medieval church, St Mary's, which retains many thirteenth-century features including the remains of the original chancel and a fragment of a wall painting. Two small brass portraits commemorate Edith and Elizabeth Wylde 'who died virgins' in 1508. Near the church are two fine early eighteenth-century houses, The Homestead and Strawberry House. Another attractive house from that period, The Grange, overlooks Barnes Common, as does the Convent of the Scared Heart, built in the eighteenth and nineteenth centuries.

Beddington Map 3 Bb

Remnants of Beddington's long history still survive. It is believed to have existed as a village in Norman times. The local manor, Beddington Place, was the the seat of the influential Carew family for over 400 hundred years from 1349. The magnificent house, rebuilt by Sir Nicholas Carew in the 1530s and greatly altered in the mid eighteenth century, now houses Carew Manor School. Queen Elizabeth I was entertained here in the enormous hall which is over 60 feet long and 32 feet wide and has a fine hammer beam roof. Another important feature is the vast orangery wall which stretches for nearly 200 feet and is said to have enclosed the first orange plantations in this country, producing excellent fruit until the trees were destroyed by frost in 1739. During a good year a crop of up to 10,000 oranges was reputed to have been produced here. The original orangery was planted in Elizabethan times by Sir Francis Carew with seeds thought to have been brought back from Florida by Sir Walter Raleigh, who married a niece of the Carews and was a frequent visitor to the house.

Legend has it that Raleigh is in fact buried, not at Westminster Abbey, but here, in Beddington Park in the ancient church of St Mary's. This perpendicular building was rebuilt by the Carews in the late-fourteenth century but fragments date from as early as the eleventh century. There are many monuments

B

and brasses in memory of the Carew family, including a brass to Sir Nicholas who died in 1432 and an alabaster monument to Sir Francis who died in 1611. The font is of Purbeck marble and dates from the thirteenth century. In 1869 the church was well-restored and decorated. At this time the William Morris Company provided a fine screened organ gallery with painted decoration, giving the impression of a medieval minstrels' gallery.

Beddington developed from a village dominated by its manor into a small manufacturing town, reaching its peak in the early nineteenth century. It is now part of London and the small town has been overwhelmed by suburban development.

Betchworth Map 4 Aa

This attractive village contains several fine old buildings, with its newer additions blending perfectly. The old houses include sixteenth-century Old Mill Cottage; the Dolphin, an inn dating from 1700; and Old House, a fine eighteenth-century Georgian building. A group of delightful cottages stand near the church, many of them dating from the seventeenth century or earlier and facing attractive old barns.

The church of St Michael was established in the mid-thirteenth century with earlier Norman segments dating from the eleventh century. Sadly it was restored in 1851 and again in 1870, resulting in the destruction of a Norman tower. Inside, some of the arches are Norman and there is a brass to Thomas Wardysworth, the vicar, who died in 1533.

The village manor house, Betchworth House, was rebuilt in 1808 in the Georgian style. Its grounds spread to the south of the village. Another interesting old house is Broome Park, which has a nineteenth-century front imposed on an older building. This was the home of the royal surgeon Sir Benjamin Brodie, one of the most distinguished doctors in England during the nineteenth century and President of the Royal College of Surgeons. It was Brodie who treated the Prime Minister Sir Robert Peel when he was thrown from his horse. Another of his prestigious patients was Isambard Kingdom Brunel. The famous engineer accidentally swallowed a coin when showing conjuring tricks to children and Brodie is said to have placed Brunel on a revolving frame, turning him upside down before dislodging the coin from his throat.

Bisley Map 1 Bb

Bisley is famous for the rifle shooting competitions held on the nearby heath by the National Rifle Association. The major international competition each year is for the Queen's Prize. The village has an old church which stands apart from the other buildings. St John Baptist dates from the thirteenth century and one of its oldest features is the church bell, given to Bisley by the monks of Chertsey Abbey in the thirteenth century. Inside, the lovely pulpit is Jacobean and the other outstanding feature is the 500-year-old wooden porch.

Bletchingley Map 4 Ab

This delightful village stands high above the Weald with a long and colourful history. The name Bletchingley is thought to originate from the bleaching process which used local deposits of fuller's earth, or heated clay, for decolorizing and fulling cloth. Bletchingley was a Saxon settlement of some importance, taken over by the Normans. A fine castle was built here in the twelfth century. Virtually nothing remains of **Bletchingley Castle** since a destructive battle was fought here during the

B

struggles between Simon de Montfort and Henry III. Seeing the peaceful village today it is hard to imagine its medieval manor and grand castle standing at the centre of a prosperous market town. Until the reforms of 1832 Bletchingley was a borough in its own right.

Much remains however in the way of fine old buildings. The most outstanding is the church of St Mary, which the Normans built first and was later refashioned in the Perpendicular style in the thirteenth century. Despite restoration much remains from both those periods. Dominating the interior is a magnificent monument, described by Nikolaus Pevsner as 'one of the most splendid early eighteenth-century monuments in the country'. It was designed by Richard Crutcher for Sir Robert Clayton, once Lord Mayor of London, who created the monument in honour of his wife in 1705. Lifesize carvings of husband and wife are elaborately carved on each side of the monument. Their only child who died as a baby in 1669 is also featured, as well as crying cherubs. So dominating is this monument, that it is easy to miss some of the church's other treasures. These include some fine brasses, dating from the fifteenth century.

Church Walk, beside the church, has some delightful old sixteenth-century buildings. The Whyte Hart Inn which stands on the attractive High Street also dates from the sixteenth century. An inn has always stood here since 1388.

Box Hill   Map 4 Aa

Box Hill (Country Parks) is one of the most famous beauty spots in southeast England. It is a high point on the North Downs offering spectacular views, especially to the south over the Weald and the Mole valley. The name comes from the box trees which used to grow densely there. Certain areas of the hill still contain large numbers of trees. Much of the area is controlled by the National Trust although certain parts have been used for caravan sites. It is usually crowded on fine summer weekends since it is a popular place to visit from London.

Box Hill has long been regarded as a beauty spot. It is the setting for one of the most memorable scenes in Jane Austen's *Emma*. Mrs Elton organizes a picnic excursion to the lovely viewpoint. John Keats the poet also appreciated it and wrote that he 'went up Box Hill this evening after the moon'.

The National Trust has created a field-study centre here at **Juniper Hall** (Field Study) which was once a refuge for French emigres fleeing the Revolution. Talleyrand was among them, as was Madame de Stael and General D'Arblay, who met Fanny Burney the novelist there and later married her. Juniper Hall enjoys a peaceful rural setting in a wooded valley near Box Hill and Mole Gap. The centre runs courses for the beginner and specialist alike, spanning natural history, art, photography, biology, history and architecture.

Bramley Map 2 Ac

The village grew up from being a tiny hamlet when the railway arrived in 1865. Its church dates from Norman times and has some thirteenth-century features.

The surrounding countryside, cut by delightful lanes, is a joy to explore. There are some interesting old buildings in the area. The most notable is Snowdenham Hall, a Victorian house south of the village. To the north is Unstead Manor House which dates from 1780. To the north also is Little Tangley, a Victorian house which was slightly altered by Edwin Lutyens in 1899. Millmead, close to the village, is a Lutyens house, built in 1904 for Gertrude Jekyll, the historian, painter and landscape gardener who was both a patron and a colleague of Lutyens. Her parents moved to the village of Bramley when she was a child and she lived there for 20 years. Gertrude Jekyll originally laid out the garden at Little Tangley.

Brockham Map 4 Aa

This charming village stands against a backdrop of Box Hill. The handsome parish church was designed by Benjamin Ferrey in 1846. Ferrey's church was created for its setting beside a most beautiful village green, enhancing the lovely group of buildings, grass and trees. During the summer months Brockham Green becomes the perfect English country cricket pitch. Cricket has been part of the village's life for over a hundred years; matches here are famous for both the setting and the quality of play and even the legendary W.G. Grace took part.

Brockham also has fine old buildings including seventeenth-century cottages and attractive farm buildings. It stands beside the river Mole and its name is said to derive from an old word for badgers.

Byfleet Map 1 Bc

The old village is now mainly a site for modern development but it has some fine old buildings. The church of St Mary has ancient origins and was rebuilt in the Early English style in about 1290. Its lovely interior contains fragments of a very old wall painting, a Jacobean font and a 500-year old brass to Thomas Teylar. At the centre of a delightful group of old buildings is the seventeenth-century brick Manor House. It was rebuilt in 1686, incorporating materials from the existing building, once a Jacobean hunting lodge which itself replaced an older lodge used by James I and later owned by Queen Anne.

C

Christopher Wren, the architect of St Paul's, signed the authorization to rebuild in 1686 and the elegant simplicity of the house echoes his work. Also part of the group is an eighteenth-century mill and an adjoining Georgian Mill House.

Carshalton Map 3 Bb

This is another of Surrey's old settlements which has become a London suburb, but an exceptionally attractive one at its centre. Here is a string of natural ponds linked by bridges and surrounded by trees. The river Wandle which flows through Carshalton enhances the town's charm. There are many delightful old buildings in this lovely waterside setting and in the streets around.

The most outstanding house, overlooking the ponds, is Carshalton House. It was built between 1696-1713 and later given a magnificent interior and landscaped gardens, only a section of which remain. All Saints church was rebuilt in the late nineteenth-century to an excellent design which incorporated the medieval tower with its eighteenth-century spire. The grand interior contains some outstanding monuments and brasses from as early as the fourteenth century.

Chaldon Map 3 Bb

Chaldon church contains one of the best preserved and most interesting wall paintings in the country. It has been named 'Ladder of Salvation' and was discovered during restoration work in 1869 beneath layers of whitewash. Above it is the oldest feature in the church, an early Norman window. Most of the remaining small flint building dates from the twelfth and thirteenth centuries. The wall painting was probably the work of monks and dates from about 1200. It precedes Dante's *Inferno* but depicts similar

C

themes. The harsh and vivid painting forms four sections with the ladder to heaven dividing the centre. The two lower frames portray hell, with fierce and massive devils stirring a cauldron of naked bodies. The seven deadly sins are shown beside the tree of good and evil. Above is purgatory, with further horrors, where two sections are divided by angels leading the righteous to heaven, itself represented as a cloud at the top of the ladder with a small motif of Christ at its centre. This is the only example of Norman art in existence in Britain in such good condition.

Another historic feature of the church is its 700-year-old bell, one of the oldest in Britain and certainly the oldest in Surrey. An interesting feature which is easy to overlook is the elaborately inscribed tablet on the north side of the chancel. It is not obviously a memorial to a particular person, but is dated 1562 and carries a simple sermon calling for goodwill towards the poor and need, for 'The cry of the poore is extreme and very sore'.

Chertsey Map 1 Ac

Chertsey is an old market town on the Thames whose name was first recorded in the Abbey Charter of A.D. 675 as 'Cerotsage' or 'the island of Cerotuse', stemming from the Latin. On the site of the Benedictine Abbey, founded in A.D. 666 by Frithwald of Surrey, the town began to flourish. This influential and prosperous religious order, one of the earliest centres of Christianity in England, wielded considerable power over the immediate area both economically, historically and politically until its Dissolution in 1533. The stones were then transported by Henry VIII to build nearby Oatlands Palace and Hampton Court for Cardinal Wolsey. All that remains of the Abbey today are a few stones, fragments of the Abbey Church and three ancient fishponds in the orchard just north of the Staines Road. Excavations in the nineteenth century unearthed some beautiful encaustic tiles and stone coffins, now displayed in **Chertsey Museum** in Windsor Street and **Guildford Museum**.

At the centre of the town the church of St Peter retains a 600-year-old chancel and medieval bell tower. One of its six bells survives from the same abbey and still sounds the curfew from Michelmas to Lady Day. This same bell is said to have tolled the knell for Henry VI when his body was secretly brought to Chertsey after he had been murdered in the Tower of London. The local legend of Blanche Heriot and her desperate feat to save the life of her sweetheart is also echoed by the bell. During the Wars of the Roses her lover was sentenced to die at curfew and in her anguish Blanche clung heroically to the clapper of this old bell to postpone the dreaded hour, in the hope that a pardon would be granted.

Across the river on the south side by Chertsey Meads is the seven-arched eighteenth-century bridge. This is a good spot to wander round the boats, tearooms or explore the Orchard Gardens, fishponds and abbey grounds. On the northern fringe of the town is a well-known beauty spot which has featured in eighteenth-century literature, St Anne's Hill, commanding views across to Runnymede and Windsor Castle. Unfortunately the countryside has been scarred by motorways but on a fine day it is claimed that you can see St Paul's. St Anne's Hill was the home of Whig politician Charles James Fox and although the original house no longer exists, its beautiful parkland studded with cedars, woodlands and nature trails is open to the public. Within the grounds are some of the original buildings, including Fox's Tea House, built in 1794 with gothic arches and imitation stalactites lending a grotto effect.

C

Another frequent visitor to Chertsey was Charles Dickens, who reputedly staged the burglary in *Oliver Twist* at Grogmore House.

To the northwest of Chertsey, within easy reach of the Thames and London, is Thorpe. Here the innovatory 400-acre, **Thorpe Park** (Unusual Outings) created by Leisure Sports Ltd., has become an important centre for watersports.

Chessington Zoo   Map 3 Ba

This was originally called Burnt Stub Zoo after the old house in the lovely grounds where the zoo is situated. The house is now the adminstrative centre and contains a restaurant. The first building here, which dated from 1348, was destroyed by fire during the Civil War in 1648. Later that century a new house was erected on the site of the 'burnt stub', hence its name. Part of the present building is early nineteenth century but considerable alterations were later made in the Jacobean style. Another fire broke out in this aptly named building in 1919 and it was further damaged during the Second World War.

Chessington Zoological Gardens (Zoos) has a large collection of animals, kept mainly in paddocks but with several smaller enclosures, including gorillas, orang-utans, penguins and a wide variety of exotic birds. The gardens cover over 65 acres and sections are landscaped. Of particular interest to children is the collection of rare domestic animals which can be handled. During the summer months there is also a fun fair, a model railway and a circus performs under a big top.

Chiddingfold   Map 2 Bb

The Normans introduced glass-making to this area in the early thirteenth century and Chiddingfold was a major centre for the industry until the beginning of the seventeenth century. The glass made here was internationally famous for its quality and colour. It was used for some of England's most magnificent stained-glass windows. The glass was made from local sand and charcoal created from burning the trees of this densely wooded countryside. The large and pretty village still stands amidst fine forests, now in the care of the Forestry Commission who are reintroducing large plantations of English oak to the district. Another industry connected with the woodlands is the ancient craft of carving walking sticks which still continues in the district today using specially cultivated ash and chestnut trees. The major industry which replaced glassmaking from the seventeenth century, was iron made from local Wealden ore. Weaving was also important in the village.

A delightful vignette is formed around the village green with its pond and surrounding tile-hung cottages, dating from as early as the seventeenth century, backed by mature trees. There are many historic buildings in the village and the surrounding countryside. One of the oldest buildings is the Crown Inn. There is some dispute as to its history with claims that it is the oldest inn in England, first established in 1285. An inn was certainly situated on this site in the fourteenth century and a title deed dated 1383 hangs inside as proof. The medieval building has an impressive king post roof and the timbers were revealed on the exterior in 1940 when traditional Surrey hung tiles were removed. The boy king, Edward VI, is said to have stayed at the inn in the sixteenth century when he passed through the village en route for Cowdray House, accompanied by an entourage of 4,000.

Fragments of the church date from as early as the thirteenth century but it was heavily restored in

C

1869. Inside is an interesting window made up of 427 segments of locally-made glass dating from medieval times and showing the full scope of texture and colour in Chiddingfold glass.

Half a mile south of the village are the fine woodland gardens of **Ramster** (Gardens) studded with rhododendrons, azaleas, camellias, magnolias, trees and shrubs.

Chilworth See Guildford

Chobham Map1 Bb

Chobham Common (Country Parks) remains a vast expanse of open land in an expensive residential area. Its barren heathland, rare in this part of England, is now partly restricted for use as an army testing ground. Chobham has retained its village character with many fine historic buildings at its centre and many more to be found in the surrounding district. Apart from the infertile common, this was rich farming land and some of the most impressive buildings are farm houses with a few grand homes.

St Laurence church dates from the eleventh century and has sections from many later periods. It was heavily restored in the Victorian era.

Compton Map 2 Ab

This attractive village was the home of Victorian artist George Frederick Watts. He was a popular painter in his day and a friend of many pre-Raphaelite artists though himself not an artist in their style. Watts married the actress Ellen Terry before she became famous, when she was just 17 and he was 47. After a short time they parted and Watts did not marry again until he was 69. The **Watts Gallery** (Art Galleries) contains a broad selection of his work including sculpture. The gallery was specially built in 1903, a year before Watt's death. His wife, Mary Fraser-Tyler, designed a mortuary chapel for her husband which can be visited. It is an extraordinary creation, built in red-brick with intricate Celtic and Romanesque motifs decorating the exterior. Inside it is richly decorated in the art nouveau style with linked angels and ornate flower and stem motifs. The whole is decorated in deep colours covering the domed mortuary.

Compton's church of St Nicholas contains an extremely rare feature in that it has a two-storey chancel, something almost unknown in British or even European churches. Neither theologians nor architects can account for its purpose. The ancient building is thought to date from Saxon times. The Romanesque additions which formed the upper storey in the chancel were undertaken in the twelfth century and include woodwork believed to be amongst the earliest of its kind ever done in this country. There are many other Norman features in the church and the eleventh-century tower has a fourteenth-century shingled spire.

Cranleigh   Map 2 Bb

Cranleigh is something between a large village and a small town. The main street is lined with maple trees lending it a French atmosphere. They were planted by Canadian servicemen who were stationed here during the First World War. Although most of the buildings were erected during the last two centuries, it is an old settlement, once a centre for the Wealden iron industry. Its oldest buildings are farmhouses on the outskirts and, of course, the church.

St Nicholas dates mainly from the early fourteenth century but has many Norman features, including

C

the nave pillars, one of which incorporates a cat's head with holes for eyes and said to be the model for Lewis Carroll's famous Cheshire Cat. The screen which divides off a chapel is fourteenth century and there is a brass dated about 1500 commemorating a priest.

Cranleigh's cottage hospital was the first of its kind when opened in 1859. Cranleigh School, a public school founded as Surrey School, was opened a few years later in 1865.

Crowhurst Map 4 Ac

Situated close to the Kent border, this old village contains a famous and ancient yew tree over 1,000 years old. Its trunk measures over 30 feet in circumference. In the last century it was hollowed out and a room was created inside with benches and a rough table where up to twelve people could sit comfortably. While this was being done, a cannon ball was found inside, believed to date from the Civil War. The tree stands beside St George's church which is rather less ancient but dates from the late twelfth century, with many features from the thirteenth and fourteenth centuries. Fragments of the stained glass date from the fifteenth century and there are old tomb-chests with brasses. Two of the oldest are in memory of members of the Gaynesford family, John Gaynesford the elder who died in 1450 and John Gaynesford the younger who died ten years later.

Just south of the village is the local manor, Crowhurst Place, which was built for the Gaynesford family in the early fifteenth century. The attractive half-timbered building was restored in 1918. The moated manor house cannot be seen from the road but it does have an imposing gateway.

Croydon Map 3 Bb

Daniel Defoe said of Croydon in the eighteenth
century that it was 'full of citizens from London'.
Today the medieval town which grew into the
largest commercial and shopping centre south of the
capital has been incorporated into Greater London.
Its importance in medieval times stemmed largely
from the Archbishops' Palace which was located
there. Archbishop Lanfranc chose the site for a
country retreat and built the first palace in the
eleventh century. It became more important as a
church centre than other retreats in Kent and Surrey
since much of the administration of the vast areas of
church lands, including many prosperous estates,
was organized from Croydon. The church sold the
Palace in 1780 when it no longer met the needs of
the Archbishops. Some had also complained that the
place was too bleak. It fell into disrepair over the
next century and was even used as a laundry and for
other commerical enterprises. What remained of the
Old Palace (Historic Homes) became a girls' school
in 1887 and exists as such today. Sections are open
to the public, including the oldest part, the Norman
undercroft, and the magnificent banqueting hall,
built in the 1380s by Archbishop Courtenay and
rebuilt in the mid-fifteenth century by Archbishop
Stafford. Much remains from the Tudor period. The
chapel was built, it is believed, by Archbishop
Bourchier between about 1460-80, and can be
visited. The other room which is accessible is Queen
Elizabeth's bedroom where Elizabeth I stayed when
visiting on matters of state.

  John Whitgift was her archbishop for the last
twenty years' of her life. His impact on Croydon was
substantial, as any visitor to the town soon discovers,
since a school, hospital and major new shopping
centre all bear his name. Whitgift was a harsh and
authoritarian archbishop, extremely orthodox on

D

religious matters. He relentlessly persecuted Puritans and was responsible for severely restricting what was published in England. Yet he is remembered as a man of great charity who used his enormous wealth in a generous and postive way, particularly in Croydon. Here he founded the Whitgift Hospital in 1596 which served also as an almshouse. This is the second oldest building in the town and set round a quadrangle. Whitgift founded various other charities in the town one of which has links with the present Whitgift school.

Six archbishops, including Whitgift, are buried in St John the Baptist church, near the Old Palace. Not surprisingly, it is the largest parish church in the district, a building which reflects the town's past association with the church. Sadly little remains of the grand ancient church founded in the tenth century and built mainly in the fifteenth century. A serious fire gutted the building in 1867 and it was soon rebuilt to a design by Sir G.G. Scott which closely followed the original.

The provincial town was well established by the early nineteenth century, but it was in the next hundred years that Croydon was to emerge as a major centre. The population at the beginning of the nineteenth century was about 6,000 and by the turn of the twentieth century it was over 100,000. Today it is well over 300,000. During the nineteenth century Croydon's situation on the main route between London and Brighton gave it significance as the resort flourished. In 1803 the first goods railway in the world ran from Croydon to Wandsworth and passenger trains started operating from West Croydon to London Bridge in 1841. Due to excellent transport links with London the town grew as a residential centre for commuters and, particularly since the Second World War, it has been seen as the perfect location for commercial development. New

Croydon has an impressive collection of large modern office buildings, a vast town hall, a major cultural centre and all the amenities of an important provincial town. Fairfield Hall, the cultural centre, was opened in 1962, and consists of a large main hall seating nearly 2,000, the Ashcroft Theatre, named after Dame Peggy Ashcroft, and an art gallery which is used mainly for exhibitions. The Whitgift shopping centre was one of the first purpose-built, traffic-free centres in the country.

Dorking Map 4 Aa

This is perhaps the most beautifully situated town in Surrey, surrounded by magnificent countryside with Box Hill, Leith Hill and the White Downs forming a dramatic backdrop. To the northwest is **Ranmore Common** (Country Parks), a vast expanse of grass and woodlands. Dorking is an ancient market town once thought to be a stopping place on Stane Street, the Roman Road from Chichester to London, but it has sadly lost much of its old character.
Development has been particularly ruthless since the 1950s, for modern office blocks and housing have replaced what must have been some charming and historic buildings. However, the High Street is delightful, not least because of its shape, with one side higher than the other, and the hills which rise beyond either end. There are also some attractive buildings here including the White Horse Inn where a fine eighteenth-century front disguises a medieval, timber-framed building. A seventeenth-century house on North Street was formerly the King's Head Inn which Charles Dickens used as the setting for the Marquis of Granby Inn, featured in *Pickwick Papers* and described by Sam Weller as 'just large enough to be convenient and small enough to be snug'.

A number of old buildings still remain, off the

D

High Street in West Street and South Street. The fine Victorian parish church, St Martin's, has been described by Nikolaus Pevsner as Henry Woodyer's 'most important church'. His design was realized between 1868-77 and its tall spire which dominates the town, reaching a height of 210 feet, is dedicated to the memory of Bishop Wilberforce who laid the foundation stone shortly before his death in a riding accident. Another Victorian church, the Congregational Church in West Street, stands on the site of the oldest Nonconformist church in Surrey, built there in 1662. Inside is an organ originally used in the Brighton Pavilion. Another attractive church, St Martin's just east of the town, was designed in 1903 by Edwin Lutyens for what was then the village of Pixham. It was created to serve as both a church and a village hall.

One of the small commons in the town, Cotmandene, has an important place in the annals of cricket history since Caffyn learnt the game here and it was he who introduced cricket to Australia. Henry Jupp, another famous cricketer from the past, was born in Dorking and also played on the common. Dorking once boasted a grand house in Deepdene, demolished in 1968. It was the home of the Duke of Norfolk at the turn of the nineteenth century and Benjamin Disraeli dedicated his novel *Coningsby* to a later owner, Henry Hope. The book was 'conceived and partly executed amid the glades and galleries' of the estate. George Meredith, the Victorian novelist and poet, is buried in the cemetry of St Martin's church. He lived nearby at the foot of Box Hill for the last years of his life. The most famous book about the town is Sir George Chesney's fictitious 'Battle of Dorking', first published in Blackwood's Magazine in 1871. The book gives an account of how England is conquered by invading German forces. The Royal Navy fleet is destroyed by torpedoes and the final battle takes place on the hills above Dorking.

The small **Dorking Museum** has a varied display of local history and a large collection of paintings, prints and photographs, housed in the former Dorking Foundry which was built in 1825.

Dunsfold Map 2 Bc

Until about fifty years ago this was the most remote village in Surrey. Today the world has encroached much closer and although an RAF airfield is situated nearby, Dunsfold has retained its charming atmosphere. The lovely green is not the neat triangle typical of the county but a large expanse, wild in places, which provides a perfect setting for the attractive old cottages in the village. Most of the buildings are brick with tile-hanging. One of the oldest is the Rectory which dates from the fifteenth

Stepping Stones

E

century. In the area many large country houses date from the seventeenth century when Londoners fled to escape the plague.

The pride of the village is its historic church of St Mary and All Saints. Built in about 1270 it is largely intact, a rare phenomenon in this area. Victorian restoration involved only extending the chancel arch and a new vestry in the northeast section. The belfry tower is fifteenth century and was renovated though not rebuilt. The rest of the church is original including the thirteenth-century pews and font. Alterations were probably made to the porch in the sixteenth century but the door to the church could be the original, strengthened with local Wealden iron. The church is approached along a delightful line of clipped yews and a large yew stands nearby, believed to be extremely old. On an outside wall of the church three plugged holes can be seen, once used as an outlet for water after washing down the brick floors inside.

East Clandon   Map 2 Ac

East Clandon is an attractive old agricultural centre which today stands out from the suburban sprawl between Guildford and Leatherhead. It has lovely old cottages and a church dating from Norman times but with mainly medieval features.

East of the village lies **Hatchlands** (Historic Homes) built for Admiral Boscawen in 1756-7. The Admiral, known as 'Old Dreadnought', was a famous sailor in his day and among his victories he defeated the French at Lagos Bay. The epitaph, inscribed on his grave in Cornwall, explains that Hatchlands was built 'at the expense of the enemies of his country' for he used prize money gained from his battles at sea.

Admiral Boscawen should also be remembered for

his good taste. Hatchlands is a fine brick house, believed to have been built to his own design in the Palladian style whose interior he entrusted to Robert Adam, the most renowned of all eighteenth-century interior designers. When commissioned to plan Hatchlands, the first private house he worked on, Adam was only 30 and had just returned from Italy where he had studied classic buildings. Outstanding examples of his design here are the plasterwork and fireplaces, rather less flamboyant than his later work but magnificent nonetheless. Sadly the Admiral died soon after moving into Hatchlands.

The village of West Clandon has another pretty group of old cottages, some of them half-timbered. The church of St Peter and St Paul has Norman origins but was heavily restored in the nineteenth century. The village is dominated by a grand estate, **Clandon Park** (Historic Homes). Like its near

Hatchlands

E

neighbour Hatchlands it is now owned by the National Trust.

The local inn is called the Onslow Arms and a magnificent pew in the church at West Clandon also bears the name of the Onslow family, who lived at Clandon Park for generations. The original house was seventeenth century and was rebuilt for Thomas Onslow in 1713-29 by the Italian architect Giacomo Leoni. It is an outstanding Palladian building with a simple brick exterior and a truly magnificent interior. The Marble Hall consists of a spectacular two-storey entrance containing marble columns and intricately decorated marble fireplaces designed by J.M. Rysbrack. The ceiling has fine plaster modelling, including full figures with their limbs overhanging the cornices. The sculptor is believed to have been the Italian master Artari. The house contains a collection of fine antique furniture and one room, the Green Drawing Room, retains the original eighteenth-century wallpaper. Fine needlework can also be seen and the rare porcelain was bequeathed to the National Trust by David Gubbay.

Three rooms have been selected to house the **Museum of the Queen's Royal Surrey Regiment**. The displays show the history of the regiment and include medals, photographs and uniforms. Although much of the main parkland, laid out by Capability Brown, is not open, the formal gardens can be visited. An ornate eighteenth-century grotto stands beside the lawn and to the east of the house is a Maori building which could have been shipped from New Zealand by Lord Onslow, Governor of the colony from 1882-92.

East Horsley see Horsley

E

Effingham Map 4 Aa

The Howards of Effingham were a colourful local
family. It was an Effingham who crushed Wyatt's
rebellion in the sixteenth century and his son was
Sir Francis Drake's Commander-in-Chief for the
fleet which sailed against the Spanish Armada.
Howard's son became the 1st Lord Effingham, taking
his title from the manor here where the family lived
from 1550 to 1647. Their home was Effingham
Court Place of which only remnants remain as part
of Lower Place Farm.

The old church of St Laurence has retained
sections from the thirteenth and fourteenth
centuries. Its tower is eighteenth century and the
whole was greatly restored in the nineteenth century.
One of the oldest remaining features is a fourteenth-
century window in the chancel, dating according to
records from a repair of the chancel by William of

Ranmore

E

Wykeham in 1388 at a time when Merton Priory, who originally held the church, had allowed it to deteriorate.

Egham   Map 1 Ac

Egham stands on the Thames, a small town which grew from a collection of ancient villages. Inevitably, situated so close to London, it has been smothered by the suburban sprawl. John Denman, the poet who became Surveyor General at the time when Christopher Wren was working, lived here as a child and one of his most famous poems, *Cooper's Hill*, describes the view from a vantage point of that name near the town. Written in 1642, it says of the mighty Thames: 'Though deep, yet clear, though gentle yet not dull, Strong without rage, without o'erflowing full.' His father, Sir John Denman, has a finely carved monument in the parish church of St John the Baptist. He was a judge and Chief Baron of the Exchequer during the reign of James I. In 1638 he died and is depicted by the monument rising in his shroud above an open-sided chest of eerie skeletons. Another beautifully sculptured monument in the church is to his two wives. One of them, Lady Eleanor, holds her second son, the future poet.

The church was rebuilt in 1817-20 leaving nothing of the medieval original. Apart from the Denman monuments, other relics were saved from the old church including one to Robert Foster, Lord Chief Justice. He died in 1663 having lived near Egham at Great Fosters, a sixteenth-century house which still stands. The old church's porch, dating from the fifteenth century, was also saved and incorporated into the new building as a lychgate. The church has an attractive Georgian pulpit.

Just outside Egham stands what Nikolaus Pevsner describes as 'the most ebullient Victorian building in the Home Counties' - Royal Holloway College. This immense building is modelled on the Chateau de Chambord in France and was built at the expense of one Thomas Holloway, a wealthy Victorian who donated much of his fortune to various useful causes. Holloway was one of the first men to exploit publicity, promoting the pills and ointments which earnt his vast wealth. They became known throughout the world after Holloway had travelled the country selling his remedies from a wagon. He ploughed money into publicity and became so rich that during the Franco-German war in the mid-nineteenth century he was able to make a substantial loan to the government of France. Having started an almanac and established the Holloway Sanatorium at Virginia Water, he put his efforts into creating what he hoped would be the first women's university. He searched Europe for a suitable building on which to model Holloway College and having seen Chambord he sent his architect, W.H. Crossland, to France for two years in order to study and measure the chateau. Holloway then built Crossland a bungalow on the site of the university, where the architect lived for six years as the magnificent building was erected.

Holloway spent £600,000, a massive but not surprising amount when it is considered that the college measures over a third of mile in circumference. One reason for the vast size was that Holloway insisted on two rooms for each student. Holloway College was incorporated into London University and since 1965 male students have been accepted there. Inside is an important art collection which can be visited in the **Picture Gallery** (Art Galleries). Holloway bought the paintings specifically for the college and all of them within two years, between 1881 and 1883. On show is work by Turner, Millais, Gainsborough, and Landseer. An important aspect of the collection is the contemporary Victorian art which Holloway considered the best of its kind, such as Filde's 'Application for Admission to a Casual Ward' and Frith's 'Railway Station'.

Southwest of Egham **Savill Gardens** form part of Windsor Great Park. This beautiful woodland is coloured with rhododendrons, flowering shrubs and rare flowers. **Gorse Hill Manor** (gardens) has over 450 different varieties of trees and shrubs.

Epsom   Map 3 Ba

The Derby, the most famous horse-race in the world, is held on the **Epsom Downs Racecourse** (Horseracing). Racing has taken place on the Epsom Downs since the time of James I. Something very different also associated with the town is Epsom Salts which made it famous long before the first Derby was run in 1780. The salts are hepta-hydrated sulphate of magnesium; water which contained the substance was first discovered in a well on the common in 1618. Gradually the health-giving qualities of the salts were discovered and Epsom developed into a popular resort, indeed England's earliest spa reaching its height near the end of the seventeenth century. Samuel Pepys visited the village in 1667 and describes in his Diary that there was 'much company'. Charles II and all his court stayed at the King's Head, favouring the now fashionable resort. By the time Daniel Defoe passed through in 1725 the town was becoming less popular, but he noted that London merchants and their families were settling in Epsom for the summer and travelling up to London each day for work, a sign of the commuter and of Epsom's role in the immediate future.

During the eighteenth century it became a fashionable place to have a summer residence and many wealthy Londoners were attracted. As a result the town has many fine Georgian buildings, particularly in Church Street. Two of the most impressive houses here are The Cedars and Ebbisham House, both dating from the early eighteenth century. The street once had the grandest house in Epsom which was sadly demolished in 1967. Pitt Place was originally a Georgian farmhouse and then converted to a mansion for Thomas Lord Lyttleton in about 1770. Other important buildings which have survived from the Georgian period include several in the area around Woodcote Road. Amongst them are Woodcote End House built about 1770, and Woodcote Grove, dating from the late seventeenth century. Nearby is Durdans, built in 1764-8, with fine wrought-iron gates. Durdans was altered in the nineteenth century when it was the home of the 5th Earl of Roseberry. One of the oldest buildings in town is Waterloo House which dates from 1690 and is situated on the High Street.

Despite much modern development, Epsom remains an area of open spaces. **Epsom Common** (Country Parks) contains over 400 acres of grass and woodland, a sanctuary for many rare plants and wildlife. The wells which produced the Epsom Salts were situated in what is now a residential area by the common. Brochures are available to accompany marked nature trails. Part of the common has been specially protected. **Epsom Great Pond** (Nature Reserves) was originally a monastic stewpond, restored in 1976 by volunteers, and now a wildlife reserve attracting water birds such as coots, moorhens, little grebes, mandarin ducks and, in winter, pochard and tufted ducks. **Horton Country Park** is located in part of the large country estate of Horton Place where mental hospitals were established in 1900. The park offers many attractive walks through rolling agricultural landscape.

E

Esher Map 3 Ba

Esher stands on the banks of the river Mole and
contains a fine stately home and a famous racecourse
Sandown Park Racecourse (Horseracing). Behind
the attractive High Street is the town's most
interesting church, St George's, a delightful stone
building which dates from 1540. It has a shingled
bell turret made of wood and inside the roof beams
are original. This church was superseded by a
Victorian parish church designed by Benjamin
Ferrey and erected in 1853-4. King Leopold of
Belgium gave £1,000 to the building fund for the
church and inside is a grand monument to him,
erected by Queen Victoria 'in memory of the uncle
who held a father's place in her affection'.

King Leopold lived in Esher from 1816. His
home was **Claremont** (Historic Homes). The
original house on the site was built in 1708 by the
architect of Blenheim Palace, Sir John Vanbrugh for
himself. By 1717 he had sold the estate to Thomas
Pelham, who later became a prominent statesman
and took the title Duke of Newcastle, commissioning
Vanbrugh to enlarge the house. Yet this building
now no longer exists, for the next owner, Lord Clive
of India, bought it after the Duke's death in 1768,
and commissioned a new home. It is a fine Palladian
house designed by the landscape gardener Capability
Brown; a rare example of his work as an architect.
The finest room inside is the Entrance Hall with a
lovely panelled ceiling. Throughout there is
plasterwork by Henry Holland and many fine
fireplaces. Lord Clive spent a fortune on the house,
over £100,000, yet never lived there. In 1816 it was
presented to Princess Charlotte, daughter of George
IV, the Prince Regent, and the wife of Prince
Leopold, later to become King Leopold. Sadly he
was soon to live there alone for the princess died in
childbirth in 1817. There is a memorial to her in the

old church of St George's. One of the rooms in Claremont on show is Princess Charlotte's room. Prince Leopold stayed on in the house and his niece, Princess Victoria, visited on many occasions. Even when she became Queen her affection for her Uncle Leopold continued and for the first ten years her birthday was spent with him at Claremont. After the revolution of 1848, the exiled French monarch, Louis Philippe, moved to the house and there he died. It is now a school for girls.

A house designed by Capability Brown can be expected to have beautiful grounds and **Claremont Landscaped Garden** is as big an attraction as the house. In fact these gardens predate the house and were first established by Vanbrugh when he owned the site. William Kent added a lake with an island, a temple and grotto. The gardens have been recently restored to their former glory and are crossed by delightful paths and avenues. The rhododendrons are particularly abundant and there are also interesting specimen trees.

Esher once had another important and grand home, Esher Place, built in the fifteenth century for Bishop Waynflete of Winchester as a staging-post for pilgrims en route for London. All that remains is the gatehouse. It was destroyed after many alterations by successive owners, including the Duke of Newcastle and Sir Richard Drake, an attendant at the court of Elizabeth I and kinsman of Sir Francis Drake. Spanish prisoners taken at the Armada were held at Esher Place. The present building dates from the end of the nineteenth century.

Ewell Map 3 Bb

The old settlement here grew up around natural springs. The Romans found it a convenient place to establish an army post and Roman remains have been excavated in the town. All that remains of

E

Ewell's medieval church is its tower which dates from the fifteenth century. A replacement was built in 1848, St Mary, designed by Henry Clutton. There are brasses commemorating the deaths of two sixteenth-century ladies inside, and a brass to a couple who died in 1721.

Two major pre-Raphaelite painters found the scenery at Ewell inspiring. Sir John Millais painted the weeping willow by the Hogsmill River in his 'Death of Ophelia' and Holman Hunt his 'Light of the World' in the town. Hunt's picture hangs in St Mary's church.

Henry VIII built a magnificent palace, Nonsuch, in Ewell, created to rival the grandest residences in Europe and Britain, in particular Wolsey's Hampton Court. Nonsuch was twice the size of its rival and an extravagant, spectacular building in the style of the French Renaissance. Master craftsmen were brought in from Europe to decorate intricately both the outside and inside. Henry did not live to see his finest building completed. It was first used by the Earl of Arundel in 1556, eighteen years after the building was started. In 1592 it was sold to Elizabeth I and she used Nonsuch as one of her main residences for many years. Charles II sailed back to England during the Reformation on ship named 'Nonsuch' after the royal estate, but he gave the palace away in 1669 and following this it was slowly dismantled. The lovely expanse of **Nonsuch Park** (country Parks) now surrounds another house, Ewell Castle, built in 1810-14. Less dramatic but of grand proportions, it stands nearer the town than Henry VIII's Nonsuch.

Other notable old buildings in Ewell include a lovely eighteenth-century Mill House with its outbuildings. There are many fine eighteenth-century buildings such as Well House in Church Street and two in Spring Street, Chessington House and Spring House. Another important historic building, Bourne Hall, stood on the High Street until 1962 when it was destroyed despite much protest. The grand old house dated from 1775. It was replaced by a domed circular building which adopted the same name and houses **Bourne Hall Museum.** Its small collection consists of bygones from the Ewell and Epsom area including costumes, toys and early photographs. There is also an art gallery with a continuous exhibition programme.

As well as the beautiful grounds of Nonsuch Park, there is a grassy, tree-lined meadow **Hogsmill** (Country Parks) to the north of the town which makes for pleasant walking.

Ewhurst Map 2 Bc

This pleasant village has retained its character despite modern development. The church of St Peter and St Paul is Norman and extremely attractive. The tower was rebuilt after it collapsed in 1838, but as with the other restoration work carried out in Victorian times, it does not detract from the original. The Norman door was uncovered this century.

There are several fine old cottages and houses in the village and closeby, on the hills to the north, are some interesting Victorian and Edwardian houses. They lie near Pitch Hill which is steep enough to attract climbers and provide spectacular views from its top.

Farnham Map 2 Aa

Farnham is one of Surrey's most historic and attractive towns. With a fine castle and many well-preserved streets lined with old buildings, it is a

F

lovely place in which to wander. There are two excellent museums and, southwest of the town, an impressive bird park **Birdworld** (Zoos).

The settlement here is ancient and was established in prehistoric times. Two of southern Britain's most important trackways, the major routes across the country in early history, pass through the settlement: the Pilgrim's Way and Harrow Way. The Romans utilized the settlement and remains have been found here of their buildings. The manor of Farnham was owned by the Bishops of Winchester from the seventh century until 1927. They built first a residence and then a castle to protect the town as it developed into a centre for agriculture. From medieval times until the seventeenth century its market was of great importance particularly for corn and wool trading. During the Civil War Farnham was a nucleus of great activity and its castle was won and lost by both sides several times. During the

The Mill, Elstead

eighteenth century many fine Georgian houses were erected and medieval residences given new fronts. The railway arrived in 1849, but since it was situated too far from London to become a commuter town, Farnham has remained a thriving country centre.

Farnham Castle Keep (Castles) and **Bishop's Palace** (Church Buildings). Built in the twelfth century by Henry de Blois, the conqueror's grandson, a brother of King Stephen and Bishop of Winchester from 1129-1171, the original tower was destroyed by Henry II in 1155. The strong keep was built later during the same century, in order to provide defence for the town. Yet the castle's domestic purpose, as a grand palace for the Winchester Bishops, was not forgotten. The living quarters were arranged below the keep and around a courtyard, a departure from the usual Norman castle layout. The basic plan has not altered since the twelfth century though the buildings were altered during the Tudor and Elizabethan periods and at the Restoration, in the seventeenth century, Bishop Morley organized extensive modernization but without changing the basic style and proportions. This was necessary following the damage inflicted on the castle during the Civil War. The keep had been partly dismantled under Cromwell's orders and it remained in ruins. It is now in the care of the Department of the Environment and can be visited separately from the main building. The latter section of the castle reverted to being a Bishop's palace rather than a fortified stronghold.

The great hall was refurbished with a magnificent new interior by Bishop Morley. The walls were raised and a vast fireplace installed. The kitchens leading off from the hall were not greatly altered in the seventeenth century and became a dining hall. The Old Chapel was restored by Morley but is basically Norman. It has twelfth-century windows

F

and the aisle was built in 1254. Another chapel was rebuilt in the seventeenth century, the Bishop's Chapel, and the magnificent carving inside was the work of master woodcarver Grinling Gibbons. The striking tower which stands at the castle's entrance was built by Bishop Waynflete in about 1470. Elizabeth I was just one royal figure to visit the espiscopal palace, when she warned the Duke of Norfolk against marrying Mary Queen of Scots.

The castle transferred to the diocese of Guildford in 1927 and continued as a residence for Bishops of Guildford until 1956. It now houses the Centre for International Briefing.

The atmosphere of Farnham is Georgian with even modern development keeping strictly to formal eighteenth-century style. Castle Street is particularly impressive. It contains many excellent Georgian, as well as a few older buildings, including the Windsor Almshouses built in 1619 for 'eight poor, honest, old and impotent persons'. The town hall stands on the corner of Castle Street. This new building, erected in 1930-34, replaced a Victorian one and is neo-Georgian, in keeping with its situation. The architect was Harold Faulkner who also restored the sixteenth-century Bailiff's Hall in The Borough.

Another sixteenth-century building, Vernon House in West Street, was given a new facade in the early eighteenth century and stands close to an attractive Georgian house, Sandford House, built in 1757. Willmer House, next door, stands out from its Georgian neighbours. Its front is regarded as one of the finest cut brick facades in the country, an intricate design which required enormous skill from the craftsmen who built it in 1718. Willmer House now contains **Farnham Museum**, laid out in a magnificent interior of finely carved oak and pine panelling. Displays cover the history of Farnham and district, eighteenth century furniture and paintings.

Farnham's most famous son is William Cobbett, the reformer and radical writer best remembered for his *Rural Rides*. He was born here in 1763 and the family home, then a farm, is now the William Cobbett pub.

Beside the River Wey to the southeast of Farnham stand the ruins of the first Cistercian monastery built in England, **Waverley Abbey** Church Buildings). It was founded in 1128 by the Bishop of Winchester, William Giffard, and occupied from the mid-twelfth century by monks from Normandy. The original church building suffered flood damage and a new building was started in 1203. This large and magnificent church took over 70 years to complete but lies in ruins today. The abbey was dissolved in 1536. The remains are extremely picturesque, standing in a lovely setting Sir Walter Scott was greatly inspired by Waverley during his research of a

Antique Shop

G

Life of Swift and named his first historical novel after the abbey. In *Sir Nigel* Conan Doyle gives a colourful description of life in a Cistercian Abbey.

Overlooking the abbey ruins is Waverley House, originally designed by Colen Campbell in about 1725 but rebuilt later that century. After this house was destroyed by fire in 1833 the present building was erected in the classical style.

A popular beauty spot south of Farnham is **Frensham Ponds** (Bird Watching). Great Pond, to the south of Frensham village, is really a lake, popular for sailing in summer. Little Pond, to the east of the village, is more secluded. Both are owned by the National Trust, as is much of the surrounding heathland, creating **Frensham Country Park**. A wide variety of animal and plant life can be enjoyed here, one of the few remaining areas of heathland in Surrey, particularly known for its heather and water birds. The area is often crowded in summer, especially at weekends, attracting some 250,000 visitors each year.

Also south of Farnham are the **Birdworld** (Bird Reserves) zoological bird gardens and aquarium. The birds are displayed in paddocks or large aviaries in which the natural habitats of the various breeds have been created. Of particular interest is the 'Sea-Shore Walk' where waders and seabirds can be seen on an impressive mock beach against which a false sea splashes. The largest inhabitant of the park is Connie 'Condor', an enormous bird from the South American Andes with a six-foot wingspan. The varieties of birds range from brightly coloured parrots to sprightly penguins. Birdworld also contains an aquarium, Underwater World, displaying beautiful tropical fish; there is also a shark tank.

Closer to Farnham is the **Old Kiln Agricultural Museum**, near the village of Tilford. Set in ten acres of countryside, the museum is laid out in old farm buildings and paddocks. There are farm implements and agricultural machinery from over the last hundred years. There are a wheelwright's shop and a working blacksmith's, also carts, wagons and horse-drawn ploughs, hand tools and yard machinery, a hop press and dairy equipment. A picnic site next to the shop sells fresh farm produce, and a woodland walk can be enjoyed in the arboretum.

Godalming Map 2 Ab

This is another medieval town and centre for the local cloth industry. It was also a staging post on the London to Portsmouth road and had several old inns amongst its historic buildings which date back to the sixteenth century. The King's Arms is the only one which is still an inn. The grand building was rebuilt in 1753. Peter the Great of Russia dined there in 1689, and a later Tsar, Alexander I, visited the inn in 1816.

The church of St Peter and St Paul dates from Saxon times with rebuilding and additions over the centuries. Restoration carried out in 1879 was extensive. There are fragments of Norman carvings on a tomb inside. The Phillips Memorial Cloister on the north side of the church was built in 1913 as a monument to Jack Phillips. He was the heroic wireless operator on the tragic first voyage of the ocean liner *Titanic* who continued to send out an SOS message until the boat finally sank.

The building which dominates the town centre is the attractive Market Hall, or Old Town Hall; known as the 'Pepper Pot' and built by local architect John Perry in 1814. The nickname comes from its domed cupolas and the stucco, octagonal building has an open arcade onto the High Street. It now houses the **Godalming Museum** with a collection relating to the history of Godalming and southwest Surrey. The High Street's other historic

G

buildings include two sixteenth-century, timber-framed houses; The Square, an early sixteenth-century tile-hung house; and the fine King's Arms coaching inn. Delightful cottages dating from the sixteenth and seventeenth centuries can be seen in Mint Lane and the adjoing Mill Lane, which also contains the eighteenth-century Friends' Meeting House and an old mill beside a stream.

On the outskirts of Godalming is Charterhouse School which moved here from Finsbury in London in 1872. The school for boys was founded in 1611 by a wealthy coal merchant. The handsome Bargate-stone building into which the school moved in 1872 was designed by P.C. Hardwick and there have been several additions since. The Great Hall was completed in 1885 and the War Memorial Chapel, erected in remembrance of Old Carthusians who died in the First World War, was designed by Sir Giles Gilbert-Scott and opened in 1927. There have

The Granary

been further modern additions including an art block built in 1958. Among the famous old-boys of this distinguished public school are John Wesley, William Makepeace Thackeray, Sir Max Beerbohm and R. Vaughan Williams.

South of the town is **Winkworth Arboretum** (Gardens), founded in the early 1940s by Dr William Fox who then owned this land. He planted a wide range of rare and beautiful trees and shrubs around a lake on what was previously scrubland. Dr Fox donated his arboretum to the National Trust in 1952. Delightful walks can be taken through the parkland which is particularly colourful in spring, when bluebells are abundant.

Busbridge Lakes (Nature Reserves) comprise 37 acres of parkland, lakes and nature trails just half a mile southwest of Godalming. There is a sanctuary for over 80 species of exotic waterfowl and birds.

Godstone Map 4 Ac

Despite its situation on a major road, Godstone has remained a lovely village. The green has a pretty pond and is surrounded by mature trees. This provides a perfect setting for club cricket in the summer months. William Cobbett was impressed by the village and his *Rural Rides* describes the White Hart inn, a reference in fact to Godstone's Clayton Arms, a fine timber-framed building from the sixteenth century. Another old inn in the village is the Bell Hotel which was rebuilt in the eighteenth century. The village's growth must be attributed to its position on the ancient Roman Road from Lewes to London, which conveyed iron from industries in the Weald.

The families of two of England's most famous diarists, John Evelyn and Samuel Pepys, lived in the area and there is a black and white marble monument to Sir John Evelyn, a relative of the

G

diarist, in St Nicholas church. Sir Gilbert Scott, the
Victorian architect who designed the Albert
Memorial, lived outside the village in a fine
Georgian house, Rooksnest, now a school. He was
responsible for renovating the Norman church in
1873. St Nicholas stands apart from the village in a
district known as Church Town. Scott also built the
almshouses near the church, in a quaint but
attractive Tudor style which blends well with the
church.

Great Bookham Map 3 Ba

The focal point of the delightful village is its lovely
medieval church of St Nicholas. The tower is a
famous landmark. It dates from the twelfth century
and is weatherboarded above a flint base, topped
with a splayed spire. There are fragments of Norman
work in the church and the chancel dates from 1341
when it was rebuilt by the masons of Chertsey
Abbey for the Abbot, John de Rutherwyke. The
stained glass in the east windows is believed to be
Flemish and dates from the fifteenth century. The
windows show six scenes from the life of Christ.
There are many excellent brasses and monuments in
the church. The oldest brass dates from 1443 in
memory of Elisabeth Slyfield, and the finest
monument is to Robert Shiers who died in 1668.
The Slyfield family were lords of the manor and
gave their name to the local grand house, later
occupied by Richard Shiers.

Two important literary figures are associated with
Great Bookham. The writer Fanny Burney and the
French emigre General D'Arblay lived in the house
known as The Hermitage after their marriage in
1783. She wrote her third novel *Camilla* in the house
and during the same period she had a child, a son
born in 1785. Jane Austen was a regular visitor to
Great Bookham. She stayed at the vicarage which

once stood by the church. Jane's godfather, Samuel Cooke, was the local vicar in the early nineteenth century. He married Cassandra, the novelist's cousin of whom Jane was particularly fond. It was from Great Bookham that Jane would have visited Box Hill which she featured in a famous scene in *Emma*.

A grand mansion stands to the south of the village **Polesden Lacey** (Historic Homes). A house has stood on the site since medieval times. A fine country mansion was built there in 1631. It was bought by the playwright Richard Brinsley Sheridan in 1796. Before he took his second wife to her new home he wrote: 'it shall be a seat of health and happiness - where she shall chirp like a bird, bound like a fawn and grow fat as a little pig.' For Sheridan, Polesden Lacey was 'the nicest place, within a prudent distance of a town, in England. He used the house as his main residence until 1802.

Polesden Lacey

G

Sheridan's Polesden Lacey was destroyed after his death in 1816 and replaced by a Regency villa in 1824. The building one sees today looks rather different from the original design by Thomas Cubitt. In 1906 it was acquired by Captain Ronald Greville; his wife refurbished and extended her home, creating an atmosphere of Edwardian splendour. She was a society hostess of boundless energy and glittering associations; members of the royal family and the most fashionable people of the day would attend her famous gatherings. Mrs Greville was also a collector of beautiful things. She inherited a fine art collection, including paintings, antique furniture and tapestries from her father, the brewing millionaire William McEwan. She added art treasures to these throughout her life, so the house is particularly noted for the objets d'art inside. In some rooms her flamboyant personality is reflected in the decor, but every room has been created with exquisite taste. The Drawing Room is particularly extravagant with painted ceilings, French Rococco fireplaces and ornate wall mirrors. Another outstanding feature of the house is the reredos from one of Christopher Wren's London churches, St Matthew, in Friday Street. The ornamental alter screen was saved when the church was demolished in 1881 and at Polesden Lacey became panelling for the entrance hall.

1,000 acres of landscaped parkland and gardens stretch away from the broad terrace behind the house, with the trees of Ranmore Common providing a backdrop to the view. Events held at Polesden Lacey in the summer take full advantage of this setting, and these include open-air productions of Shakespeare.

Guildford   Map 2 Ab

Surrey's county town has been appreciated as one of the finest towns in the Home Counties, both in the past and as it stands today. William Cobbett described Guildford as 'The prettiest and taken altogether the most agreeable and happy looking town that I saw in my life', high praise indeed from a man who travelled England extensively when researching his *Rural Rides,* published in 1830. Nikolaus Pevsner, another insatiable traveller through England, describing every place in detail for his *Buildings of England* series, said of Guildford that it is 'one of the best old towns near London'.

Two important aspects of the town have combined to make it the lovely place it is: its long and colourful history and its topographical setting, straddling the Wey river with steep approaches on either side, providing it with hills and vistas. The name of the town is believed to derive from the fact that here was a ford across the river Gil or Gilon, the old name for the Wey. River crossings were always important and often the site for ancient settlements. This one was particularly important since it was on the route of the Pilgrim's Way. By Saxon times the settlement was well-established and the Normans, recognizing the strategic importance of the place, built a strong castle to protect the gap in the Downs, around which a town grew up. Weaving became an important industry in Kent, Sussex and Surrey during the middle ages and Guildford became the centre for dyeing and finishing the cloth produced in the surrounding villages. Blue kersey material was in great demand and produced exclusively in Guidlford. The arms of the city show wool sacks and the colour of Guildford is blue. The town always remained a busy staging post at the meeting place of two major cross-country routes. As the weaving industry slowly declined during the seventeenth century, Guildford's prosperity came from another source, the river Wey Navigation, a canal opened in 1653. It was extended to Godalming in 1763 and became a busy trade canal carrying produce up to the river Thames and so to London.

G

The mid-nineteenth century marked the height of the canal's activity, but this period also saw its sudden and final decline, for the railway had arrived in Guildford in 1845 it could not compete. Today the waterway is packed with pleasure craft and narrow boats, as visitors enjoy a peaceful day out or a holiday on the water.

Guildford is still a bustling centre for Surrey. It is a cathedral town, the see of Guildford having been established as a separate diocese from Winchester in 1927. The University of Surrey is here and Guildford has major administrative and commercial offices as well as a large shopping centre.

The modern **Guildford Cathedral** (Church Buildings) was built between 1936-54 to a design by Edward Maufe who won the commission from a competition. It is a conservative, restrained building with a powerful atmosphere and simple nobility. The interior is particularly striking with elegant arches defining the tall nave. The university buildings are also simple and unpretentious with tall towers and yellow brickwork. Battersea College of Technology became the new Surrey University in 1966 and the first new buildings for it were opened in Guildford in 1968. The academic emphasis is on science, engineering and technology.

These fine modern buildings are in sharp contrast to the Guildford of the High Street. Like the town itself, this street has been singled out for its attractive arrangement of old buildings and lovely setting. Pevsner said 'it is an almost perfect example of a bright and cheerful Home Counties' street, whose effect is that of unity-in-diversity'. Oliver Mason, in his guide to South-East England, claims that the 'High Street' is one of the most satisfying streets in the South-East, and that is a large claim'. Charles Dickens found this street the most beautiful in all England. Along its sloping path are many outstanding old buildings. At the top is the town's

Royal Grammar School which was founded by Roger Beckingham in 1509 and given a Royal charter by Edward VI in 1552. The Tudor building dates from 1553 and is still a school.

Dominating this end of the High Street is the huge gatehouse of Abbott's Hospital, a magnificent Jacobean building dating from 1619-22. Its founder was a local man and a pupil at the Royal Grammar School, George Abbot, who became Archbishop of Canterbury. The almshouses were built by him for 12 old men and eight old women. Later is was used for ten persons of each sex. Their living quarters are set around a delightful square reached beyond the gatehouse. The brick building has tall turrets and attractive chimneys. One turret facing the quad carries the bell, which was tolled for latecomers in byegone days, and there is a lovely clock which replaced a sundial in 1742. This outstanding courtyard is reminiscent of the finest university quads and its buildings are still used by those in need. The beautiful old doors, wood panelling and many other details have been well-preserved and the elegant interior contains antiques and paintings from many periods. The Banqueting Room is lined in carved oak with an intricately carved black oak fireplace depicting elements of a feast. Four standing figures represent those who will serve such fare as the boars' heads and water fowl which are carved along the top of the mantel. Below, a row of faces with open mouths, represent the guests who will consume the banquet and at the centre are the entertainers a jester, a singer and a reciter. The Monmouth Room was occupied by the Duke of Monmouth the night before he reached the Tower of London, following his defeat in the Battle of Sedgemor in 1685. On the ground floor is a small chapel with seventeenth-century Flemish stained glass, depicting the story of Jacob in detailed sections crowded with biblical figures.

G

Opposite the Abbott's Hospital is Guildford's parish church of the Holy Trinity. The oldest section is the Weston Chantry built in the mid-sixteenth century. The rest was rebuilt between 1749-63 following the collapse of the original tower. Archbishop Abbott was buried inside in 1633 and his grand monument was erected seven years later. Another man of fame buried in the church is Arthur Onslow who was Speaker of the House of Commons for 33 years and died in 1778.

A short distance down the High Street stands a fine seventeenth-century home, Guildford House, built as Child House in 1660 for a local lawyer. John Child. The interior has finely decorated plaster ceilings, pine panelling and an intricately carved staircase. The window catches are wrought iron, a delightful feature. The house was acquired by Guildford Corporation in 1957 and now houses the **Guildford House Gallery** (Art Galleries) with monthly exhibitions on show. It is also used as a meeting centre for local societies and for adult education classes.

One of the outstanding features of the High Street is the delightful clock which hangs above the road. It is attached to the old Guildhall, regarded as the best of the buildings in Guildford and taking full advantage of its situation as the focal point of the High Street. The Tudor original was given a new front in 1683. The first floor's central section overhangs the street to form a balcony with iron railings. Inside, the Courtroom is on the ground floor and above the Council Chamber. The grand gate opposite is Tunsgate, built as the entrance to the Corn Exchange in 1818. The corn market no longer exists and the gate now stands before the Tunsgate Square pedestrian shopping precinct. The High Street continues with many more attractive and historic buildings.

Quarry Street runs off the High Street and is

another very attractive road. At the end is Guildford's oldest church, St Mary's, with a flint tower believed to date from Saxon times. The outside was restored in 1862 but the interior is largely intact and dates from Norman times to the thirteenth century. Nearby is **Guildford Museum** and the headquarters of the Surrey Archaeological Society. The museum is housed in the seventeenth century Castle Arch and has a magnificent embroidery collection, rare examples of Wealden ironwork as well as displays on other aspects of Guildford and Surrey history. A special display is dedicated to the memory of Lewis Carroll. The author of the most famous of all Victorian children's books, *Alice in Wonderland* and *Through the Looking Glass*, whose real name was Charles Lutwidge Dodgson, was closely associated with Guildford. His sisters lived here at the family home, The Chestnuts, which stands near the museum on Castle Hill. The house bears an enamel plaque showing various Carroll characters, such as Alice herself, the White Rabbit and the grinning Cheshire Cat, which decorate the writer's name. Lewis Carroll was an occasional preacher at St Mary's church. He died at The Chestnuts in January 1898 and is buried in the old cemetery on the Mount; his grave is marked by a marble cross.

The museum adjoins the grounds of **Guildford Castle**, which have been laid out as attractive public gardens. Only the keep of the Norman castle remains, a solid square structure which is now no more than a shell but can be climbed and offers extensive views from its top. The castle was built in the early twelfth century on a Saxon mound which was fortified in the eleventh century. The keep tower dates from about 1170. Despite its defensive purpose, this was a grand royal residence in medieval times. Princes and princesses are believed to have spent their early years here, in a palatial royal nursery.

G

Guildford has a modern theatre, the Yvonne Arnaud Theatre, which stands on a promontory surrounded on three sides by the river Wey and was built in 1963-5. During the serious floods of 1968, the promontory became an island and much of the area was submerged under deep water, including St Nicholas church. The originally medieval building was twice moved to higher ground and rebuilt because of the threat of flooding.

Guildford has an important architectural museum, **The Brooking Collection** (Museums). This wide-ranging and important private collection of architectural features includes windows, doors, fireplaces, fanlights and decorative ironwork. It is used as a source of reference and information by those preserving old buildings and dating their features. The existing museum is limited for space and new premises have been found, but at present the collection can be viewed only by arrangement.

Loseley House

G

Just over a mile to the southwest of Guildford stands **Loseley House** (Historic Homes). This elegant Elizabethan mansion was originally larger. It was built for Sir William More between 1561-9 and has unique, carved-chalk chimneys. Inside, the Great Hall has seventeenth and eighteenth-century fittings, and some outstanding sixteenth-century features, not believed to have been originally made for the house. These include the fine wood panelling, said to have come from Henry VIII's magnificent, Nonsuch Palace which now no longer exisits. This is assumed because Sir William More was the executor of Sir Thomas Cawarden, Keeper of Nonsuch, and he may have bequeathed the fittings to More. However, there are no records to confirm that pieces from Nonsuch were incorporated into Loseley Park. The house also contains collections of antique furniture, tapestry and needlework.

Another grand home near Guildford is **Chilworth Manor** (Gardens), a rustic seventeenth-century building which was extended in the eighteenth century. Its beautiful garden includes ponds which were originally stewponds used by the monks of an eleventh-century monastery, recorded in the Domesday Book as standing on this site. The garden was laid out in the seventeenth century but its main attraction, a delightful walled garden, was added by Sarah, the Duchess of Marlborough and widow of the great Duke in the eighteenth century. The garden's terraces rise uphill and are ablaze with colourful flowers in spring. Flower arrangements can be seen in the house in April. The flowering shrubs provide an equally impressive display later in the year.

Sutton Place (Historic Homes, Art Galleries) was the English home of one of this century's most famous millionaires, the American Paul Getty, reputedly the richest man in the world. Getty was an art collector almost without equal in his time and

G

the Sutton Place Heritage Trust, which he founded, will ensure that this outstanding estate is used for cultural events including art exhibitions and music concerts as well as other special events and historical exhibitions. Both the house and gardens have been extensively restored this century, the house under the direction of Sir Hugh Casson and the gardens by Geoffrey Jellicoe. They have only recently been opened for public viewing.

Sir Richard Weston was granted the estate of Sutton in 1521 by Henry VIII but the exact date from which the house was built is not known. Weston was a favourite courtier of Henry VIII until 1542, despite his son being beheaded in 1536 for his part, allegedly the Queen's lover, in the scandals which led to the execution of Anne Boleyn. The original building was square, constructed around a courtyard but the north side was completely demolished in 1786. Now the house appears as a central core with two projecting wings carrying step gables. It is a fine example of Early English Renaissance architecture and contains a magnificent art collection including rare tapestries, paintings and outstanding stained glass in the hall which dates from the sixteenth and seventeenth centuries.

The gardens are also superb, created by Jellicoe in what has been called the greatest garden scheme since Chatsworth, with some extraordinary twentieth century elements. A sculptural wall is based on a design by Ben Nicholson, the abstract painter. A fish-shaped lake was added this century, as was the Surreal Garden and, another tribute to modern art, the Miro Swimming Pool Garden. A Paradise Garden has rose arbours, fountains and a lily moat.

South of Guildford on the Tillingbourne River is **Shalford Mill**, a restored eighteenth-century water-mill. Thanks to a mysterious group of anonymous benefactors, the mill was repaired and donated to the

National Trust in 1932. The Ferguson Gang, a 'Saintly Mafia' as they called themselves, were a set of masked gangsters who circulated the countryside delivering banknotes on a mission to preserve selected English treasures.

Ham   see Petersham

Haslemere   Map 2 Bb

Haslemere is a pleasant small town set amongst wooded hills on a high escarpment overlooking the Weald. This was once a busy town with iron, woodwork, glass and leather amongst its industries. However since the eighteenth century it has become increasingly residential and there is little industry in Haslemere today.

The town has important cultural associations. It is

The Old Watermill, Shalford

known for music with an annual **Haslemere Festival** (Events) held usually in July. The town has also attracted many writers. George Eliot (Mary Ann Evans), Conan Doyle and Alfred Tennyson lived here. Tennyson loved the town and the surrounding country. He wrote of his mother's joy in the views to be seen from Haslemere: 'You came, and looked and loved the view long known and loved by me'.

The musical associations of the town stem from a man who came to settle here in 1917, Arnold Dolmetsch. With his family he created the **Dolmetsch Workshops** (Crafts) which have specialized in making musical instruments using traditional and ancient materials and designs for nearly 70 years. Arnold Dolmetsch was dedicated to reviving old music as well as creating instruments on which to play it. He also established concerts providing a unique opportunity to hear the music of early English composers, of the Elizabethans and major European classical composers performed as it was in their day. His ancestors were instrument makers and now his family continue the tradition. Pianos, harpsichords, virginals, spinets, lutes, violas, recorders and other instruments are still made in the workshops. The Haslemere festival was established from the Dolmetsch concerts and the instruments are also occasionally played at the workshops.

Haslemere also has a celebrated museum, the **Educational Museum**. Its founder was a surgeon, Sir Jonathan Hutchinson, who established the museum in 1888. He wanted it to be a place where visitors of all ages could learn from the exhibits and have them explained clearly. This developed from his own interest in collecting botanical, geological and archaeological specimens from the surrounding countryside which he then used as the foundation for educational talks to children. The natural history section of the museum includes a magnificent display of British birds and a beehive which can be closely studied. There is a varied geology collection and a section on local prehistoric archeology. Local industrial history includes exhibits on Haslemere's iron and glass industries and there is a unique collection of peasant arts and crafts from Britain and northern Europe.

The town has an old church which was restored in 1871 but retains its thirteenth-century tower. Tennyson, who actually lived just across the Sussex border on the edge of the town, is remembered in a stained-glass window designed by Edward Burne-Jones. It depicts Sir Galahad kneeling in a small chapel where he was visited by the Holy Grail. Many of its old-style buildings are faithful nineteenth-century recreations which blend well with the town and its surroundings. Walks can be enjoyed in the woodland, much of which is owned by the National Trust.

Hindhead Map 2 Bb

The magnificent views from this lovely open countryside make Hindhead one of Surrey's outstanding beauty spots. Yet it is a place which only 150 years ago was known as dangerous and sinister. Names in the area such as Gibbet Hill, from where one of the most spectacular views in the south can be enjoyed, and the **Devil's Punchbowl** (Country Parks), a sweeping hollow, seem misplaced in this delightful scenery. Dickens described Nicholas Nickleby and his companion Smike venturing along the Portsmouth Road here, nervously remembering why this desolate place was known as Gibbet Hill. It is said that a sailor was murdered at the spot in the eighteenth century and that three men guilty of the crime were hanged in

H

chains on the hilltop until they died. William Cobbett described Hindhead as the 'most villainous spot God ever made'. One can only imagine the fears of travellers past crossing this wild area which today is appreciated as a large unspoilt open space.

Holmwood Map 4 Aa

The village is unremarkable, with two Victorian churches and pleasant buildings including a house designed by Edwin Lutyens, the Dutch House. The village, consisting in fact of North and South Holmwood, is situated beside a large expanse of forest and heathland. Through this ran Stane Street, the important Roman road between Chichester and London. The Surrey Archaeological Society have excavated a section in Redlands Wood which shows the original metalling of flint and sandstone.

In the nineteenth century a wealthy American settled here, Alfred Gwynne Vanderbilt, son of the famous millionaire. Having spent much of the last twenty years of his life in this area he died when the liner *Lusitania* was sunk by a German torpedo during the First World War in 1915. He was a hero of that tragedy. Vanderbilt organized the passengers to search for children before loading them into lifeboats. Then, unable to swim himself, he gave up his lifebelt to an elderly woman. A memorial on the A24 commemorates the gallant gentleman.

Horsley Map 2 Ac

The Horsleys, East and West, are villages between Leatherhead and Guildford, known for their lovely mature trees and surrounding woodland. East Horsley is dominated by Horsley Towers, built by Sir Charles Barry, the architect of the Houses of Parliament. Its owner was Earl Lovelace, Lord Byron's son-in-law. He was himself an engineer and

amateur architect who altered Barry's original
building considerably. As a result it is an extravagant
display of the Victorian Gothic style. A tall Rhenish
tower was added in 1858 and the extensive cloisters
a year later.

Many of the village's other buildings were also the
work of Earl Lovelace who was a fine and inventive
engineer. The church of St Martin was originally
founded in Norman times and largely built in the
thirteenth century but was heavily restored by H.
Woodyer in 1869. Inside are some fine old
monuments. A late fourteenth-century brass to
Robert de Brantingham is protected under glass.
John Bouthe, Bishop of Exeter, who died in 1478 is
also remembered by a brass, for he once ran this
parish 'wondrous well'. An impressive monument to
Thomas Cornwallis, Groom Porter to Elizabeth I,
and his wife Catherine, was erected in the 1620s.
The alabaster sculpture shows him in plate armour

East Horsley

and she is dressed in the Stuart style of the period when she died. Beneath them kneel their two sons, both of whom died when young. The local family called Snelling, who were apparently blacksmiths in the fifteenth century, are twice remembered. John and Alice Snelling are shown in a crude brass with their 11 children. Thomas Snelling has a memorial with his 13 offspring.

West Horsley also has an old church and a grand house which stand together to the east of the village. The church of St Mary is believed to have been of Saxon origin with a Norman tower and much thirteenth-century work to be seen. This includes stained-glass medallions in the windows of the chancel. A large tomb for Sir Edward Nicholas, who died in 1669, is thought to have been carved by Grinling Gibbons. The most historic monument is to Ralph Berners who was a priest and the rector of this parish. He died in 1348 and his tomb bears a fine sculpture of him in prayer with an intricately decorated canopy.

The Berners family lived at West Horsley Place before it was partially rebuilt by Henry VIII's Master of the Horse, Sir Anthony Browne. It was again enlarged and altered in the sixteenth century and the brick south front was added in about 1630. Further alterations took place in the eighteenth century. In the seventeenth century the estate was inherited by Sir Walter Raleigh's son, Carew, and legend relates that he buried his father's head here. Lady Raleigh is said to have preserved her husband's head and carried it with her in a red leather case until she died. After Carew Raleigh's death the house passed to Sir Charles Nicholas, a leading statesman under Charles I. When a later member of the Nicholas family was buried in the chapel here in 1703, it is claimed that the head of Sir Walter Raleigh was revealed.

K

West Horsley has several attractive old buildings around the church and in the village street. These include Church House which is sixteenth century, half-timbered and with an overhanging first floor.

Kew Map 3 Aa

When visiting Kew from central London the best form of transport is by boat down the Thames. The landing stage leads into the world famous **Royal Botanic Gardens, Kew** (Gardens). This delightful area beside the river was for many years a popular residence for royalty and was known for its rich soil. In the grounds of Richmond Palace nearby stood, from 1704, the Richmond Lodge which became the favourite residence of George II and Queen Caroline. The gardens were first planted and landscaped by Charles Bridgeman and then, in 1770, by Capability Brown. In 1730, George II's son, Frederick Prince of Wales, and his wife Princess Augusta, decided to build a new house for themselves at Kew. The White House was erected for them by William Kent. After the Prince's death in 1751, his widow put much of her energy into the gardens which surrounded White House. In 1759 she dedicated nine acres towards a Botanic Garden and the foundation was laid for the present Kew Gardens.

Sir William Chambers, who designed Somerset House, built a number of garden temples to house the specimen plants and many of his original buildings remain, including the exotic Pagoda built in 1761, which is ten storeys high and built mainly for decoration. Chambers visited China and built his Pagoda in traditional Chinese style. After Princess Augusta's death her son, George III, continued to take a keen interest in the gardens of White House and he placed them in the care of Sir Joseph Banks, a leading botanist who accompanied Captain Cook on his voyage to discover Australia. Botany Bay, in

K

New South Wales which was to become the landing place for convict exiles, was so-named because of Banks' recognition of the unique character of the plants he found there. Botanists from Kew went on many major expeditions, two of whom were on the *Bounty* which saw perhaps the most famous mutiny of all time. Under Banks' direction plant specimens were brought from around the world to Kew. Banks died in 1820 and the gardens were sadly neglected until a public outcry led to 14 acres of the royal pleasure gardens being dedicated to the nation in 1841. More and more of the royal parkland has been given to the Botanic Gardens over the years and they now cover more than 300 acres.

Apart from Chamber's 163-foot Pagoda, the most well-known building is the vast Palm House. The engineer for this magnificent glass and steel structure was Richard Turner and the architect was Decimus Burton. It took four years, from 1844-48, to erect the building which is 362 feet long and topped by curved glass roofs.

George II and Princess Augusta's White House was destroyed in 1822 after George III had decided to build a grander country residence nearby. It was never completed inside and was pulled down without being used in 1828. But the grandest house of all, **Kew Palace** (Historic Homes), has survived since its erection in 1631. It was originally called the Dutch House and was built for Samuel Fortrey, a London merchant of Dutch descent. It has fine brickwork and gables. George III lived there towards the end of his life and there are mementoes of him on show. Closeby is the fine Orangery which Chambers built in 1761 and was for many years the largest hothouse in the country.

Another royal residence here is **Queen Charlotte's Cottage** (Historic Homes), a delightful rustic thatched cottage built in 1772 and used as a summer house and for royal picnics. The interior has been renovated to its original style. The Botanic Gardens form such a spectacular park that it is easy to forget that this is a major scientific establishment, indeed the world's greatest botanic research institute. Large areas to the west of the gardens are given over to trees. The rest of the area is laid out in formal gardens and those plants which require specific climatic conditions are placed in the various houses, such as the Palm House, Temperate House, Australia House and many more. Specimens are brought here for identification and classification. The gardens are also used as a quarantine station for plants being sent from one part of the world to another in order to avoid the spread of damaging diseases.

At the centre of Kew village is its attractive triangular green faced by an eighteenth-century

The Palm House, Kew Gardens

K

church and many fine Georgian houses. Royal patronage in the area clearly made this a fashionable place for a country residence in the Georgian period and aristocrats lived in some of the grand homes. The church of St Anne was built between 1710-14 and lengthened in 1770. In 1850 a domed mausoleum was added for the Duke and Duchess of Cambridge who lived on Kew Green.

Kingston-upon-Thames Map 3 Aa

Now a part of Greater London, Kingston retains many administrative departments of Surrey, including County Hall. Ancient kings of Surrey lived here, hence its name meaning town of the king. That was as long ago as the seventh century so this is a truly historic settlement. It probably became established because of the fine hunting country around it and the fact that the Thames could be forded here in ancient times. The Romans would certainly have made use of a settlement here, though there is nothing to prove this. The town came into greater prominence during the Saxon period. A Saxon chapel stood in the centre and the outline of its foundations have been marked in stones. It was here that seven Saxon kings were crowned on a large stone which has now been removed from its original site and stands outside the Guildhall. The town's name is often said, incorrectly, to derive from 'King's Stone'. The first king to be crowned on the stone is believed to have been Edward the Elder, son of Alfred the Great, in A.D. 901. Athelstan, a great warrior king, was crowned here in A.D. 925 and the line continued with Edmund, Edred, Edwy, Edward the Martyr and finally Ethelred the Unready who gained the kingdom in A.D. 978.

The Normans built the church of All Saints adjacent to the Saxon chapel and they stood side by side until a disastrous event in 1729. As the church sexton and gravedigger were preparing a grave, with the sexton's daughter helping the digging, the Saxon chapel collapsed on them, killing both the men. The daughter, Hester Hammerton, was saved by a pillar which fell across the grave; the pillar is now inside the church. Despite the heavy restoration of 1862, the church retains some Norman traces as well as work of the thirteenth-fifteenth centuries. Inside are some old monuments including a brass to Robert Skerne who died in 1437 and a lovely stone memorial to Philip Meadows raised by John Flaxman in 1795. There is also a fine stained-glass west window erected in about 1865.

South of the church is the focal point of Kingston, its lively and attractive Market Place. The old town hall dominates the scene. It was built in 1840 and standing on its first floor facing outwards is a statue of Queen Anne by Francis Bird who was paid £48 for it in 1706. Across from the market is the modern Guildhall, built in 1935 and extended in 1968, before which stands the ancient coronation stone of the Saxon kings.

There are some fine old buildings in London Road, including the chapel of Kingston Grammar School, formerly Lovekyn Chapel founded in 1309. Cleave's Almshouses date from 1668. **Kingston Museum and Heritage Centre** features the work of a local nineteenth-century photographer, Eadweard Muybridge, whose moving projector or zoopraxiscope is on show as well as some of his photographs. Also displayed are archaeological finds from the Bronze Age and Saxon remains from the area. Other exhibits relate to the history and natural history of Kingston and district.

The river provides an attractive setting for the town. An old bridge, Clattern Bridge, dating from the twelfth century, crosses the Hog's Mill River.

K

The stone arched bridge which crosses the Thames was built in 1828 and widened in 1914. An aqueduct or conduit runs beneath the town and the river. It was built by Cardinal Wolsey to carry water from the springs of Combe, now a leafy suburb of Kingston, to his magnificent **Hampton Court Palace** (Historic Homes) on the other bank of the Thames. It was built for the Archbishop of York, Cardinal Wolsey in the sixteenth century who was the most powerful man in England after Henry VIII. On Wolsey's fall, Henry Tudor enlarged it and further alterations were made by Christopher Wren including the addition of an Orangery. Hampton Court is constructed around three main Courts, approached from Hampton Court, in the west, via the dried moat and Wolsey's impressive Gateway. Bade Court is the first and largest court, dating from Wolsey's time. On the east side is Ann Boleyn's Gateway leading to Clock Court. The gateway bears Wolsey's arm and motto and the famous astronomical clock. The Great Hall, built by Henry VIII stands on the north side with its fine hammerbeam roof. The third court, Wren's Fountain Court is enclosed by the main state rooms and audience chambers, including the King's Side facing south over the Privy Garden and the Queen's Side facing east over the Fountain Garden. The palace is world famous for its fine state apartments decorated with paintings by Vanbrugh, Verrio and Thornhill and outstanding tapestries. The Cumberland Suite has been recently restored, and the picture gallery has an extraordinary collection including rare Italian masterpieces. Perhaps the most important pictures are Mantegna's nine great canvases, *The Triumph of Julius Caesar*, originally brought from Mantua by Charles I. The exterior and grounds are as well-known as the opulent interior. Here are the mellow courtyards and expansive parkland. On the north side of the palace are the Tudor tennis court, the oldest place in the world where real tennis is still played, the Tiltyard Gardens and Maze; to the east is the Fountain Garden. The maze is ever-popular with visitors and an enormous great vine stands where it was first planted in 1769.

Leatherhead   Map 3 Ba

Sadly little remains of the ancient town of Leatherhead since post-Second-World-War development. A church has stood here since Saxon times and the present parish church of St Mary and Nicholas has a fine interior with many features from the twelfth and early thirteenth centuries. Fragments of medieval glass have been combined to create one stained-glass window in the north aisle. The flint tower is believed to date from the fifteenth century and the chancel arch was built at the end of the twelfth century but has been heavily restored. Handel is said to have once played the church organ.

In the graveyard lies Sir Anthony Hope Hawkins, author of *The Prisoner of Zenda* which he wrote under the name Anthony Hope. His father was the headmaster of the local boys' public school, St John's. Another literary figure connected with the town is the Tudor poet John Skelton who was Henry VIII's tutor and unofficial poet laureate. The old Running Horse Inn in Bridge Street, with parts dating from the fifteenth century, is believed to have been the inn described in his poem *The Tunning of Elynour Rummyng* which he wrote in 1517. The ale-wife, Elynour, is said to have brewed (tunning) 'noppy al' for 'travellers and tynkers, for sweters and swynkers, and all good ale drynkers'. Leatherhead has some other old buildings including attractive flint and brick cottages near the centre and eighteenth-century Sweech House, which was restored by the Local Countryside Protection Society in 1950.

L

Leatherhead Museum was founded by the local history society and is housed in a restored seventeenth-century yeoman's cottage. The exhibits relate to the history of the town and surrounding area, including Great and Little Bookham, Ashtead and Fetcham. Private collections and paintings by local artists are also sometimes on display. The Thorndike Theatre opened in 1969 on the site of an old cinema in Church Street. With seating for 562 in its ingeniously designed interior, the theatre offers a wide range of entertainment and drama. The modern Council Offices stand on the site of Kingston House where John Wesley preached his last sermon in 1781.

Leigh Map 4 Ab

'Lie', an old word for a forest clearing, was much-appreciated by Ben Jonson, a dramatist and contemporary of Shakespeare. He would come here

The Bridge over the river Mole

to relax at Swains Farm, outside the village, which still stands though greatly altered since the seventeenth century. The village is typical of the most picturesque in Surrey, clean or orderly yet with a delightful rustic atmosphere centred round the green, offset by a nice old church with a Horsham slate roof, a weatherboarded eighteenth-century inn, The Plough, attractive cottages, an ancient Priest's House and the village school. The whole is set high above the Weald which can be seen beyond the mature trees.

St Bartholomew church is perpendicular, most of it dating from the fifteenth century and unspoilt by its Victorian renovators. Inside the stained-glass by C.E. Kempe must be appreciated. Kempe was one of the best Victorian artists in stained-glass and his work can be seen in churches throughout Surrey and East Sussex. Also in the church is a brass to John Arderne, once the High Sheriff of Surrey who died in 1499, shown with his family below.

The Ardernes lived at Leigh Place, north of the church, a moated fifteenth-century house virtually rebuilt in 1810 with Gothic features. The Priest's House on the green forms a line of lovely low half-timbered buildings which stretch down the road. They have been extensively renovated and given additions, but this has not detracted from their charm.

Limpsfield Map 4 Ac

Another delightful Surrey village on the edge of the Weald, Limpsfield is surrounded by lovely countryside dotted with old farms. A broad panorama of the entire area can be seen from Titsey Hill, 900 feet above sea level to the north of the village. **Titsey Plantation** (Woodland) offers a

L

beautiful woodland walk accompanied by a leaflet, however Titsey Place and grounds are not open to the public.

The fine old church of St Peter stands off the High Street. Its oldest parts date from the late twelfth century and much of the building is thirteenth century including the nave and chancel. It is approached through a fourteenth-century lynchgate. Frederick Delius, the famous composer, was buried in the churchyard in 1934 after requesting a resting place in an English country cemetery. During the last years of his life he was blind and stricken with paralysis, but continued to work. Another gravestone remembers Florence Barclay, who died in 1921 and was a bestselling novelist.

Eugenia Stanhope is the most notorious of the cemetery's occupants. She was married to Philip Stanhope to whom Lord Chesterfield wrote the *Letters to His Son*. Philip Stanhope had been a disappointment to his father. The letters set out how Philip could become a man of the world and a perfect gentleman but they were meant for no eyes but his own. When the son died from dropsy in 1768, Chesterfield was astonished to find he had been secretly married to Eugenia and had two small sons. He provided for them and Eugenia lived in the old Manor House in the village. She had kept her husband's letters but never told Chesterfield and she sold them to a publisher as soon as she could after the old man's death in 1773. She received the handsome sum of £1,500 and the letters caused quite a stir when published.

The main village street contains many outstanding buildings. Opposite the church is the old Rectory dating from the seventeenth century. There are pretty groups of cottages and an impressive fifteenth-century hall house, **Detillens** (Historic Homes), disguised by an eighteenth-century front. Inside there are good woodwork features including inglenooks, a stately kingpost roof in an upper room, panelling and fine firebacks. Antique china and furniture are on show as well as a collection of militaria, including orders of chivalry and other military decorations. Adjacent to the house, in what was once a slaughter house, is a museum of country crafts.

The whole village stands on high ground but to the east is a ridge, higher still, and here is the area known as Limspfield Chart which was developed as a delightful garden suburb in the nineteenth century. The Chart is now Forestry Commission land open to the public and the beautiful woodland and heath make an ideal picnic spot. There is an older, seventeenth-century Mill House which once formed part of a windmill complex. Most of the other grand homes are Victorian and the church here, St Andrew's, was designed by Sir Reginald Blomfield in 1895. It contains a reredos typical of the Arts and Crafts Movement.

Lingfield   Map 4 Ac

This sizeable village is known now for the pleasant **Lingfield Park Racecourse** (Horseracing) but it achieved prominence in the fifteenth century. Sir Reginald Cobham founded a college for secular priests here in 1431. The Cobhams were an influential local family who lived at Starborough Castle, about a mile east of the village. Records show that Reginald de Cobham was given permission to crenellate his estate in 1341. Very little remains of the castle apart from the ruined bases of its once four grand towers and the moat. The castle was destroyed during the Civil War. A Victorian country house was built next to the ruins in about 1880.

Sir Reginald Cobham's college has also gone. It

L

was closed by Henry VIII during the Dissolution in 1544 and the main buildings were destroyed in the eighteenth century. One of them however remains, next to the church of St Peter and St Paul which was rebuilt in 1431 and attached to the college. The County Library is now housed in this Old Guest House of the college, dating from the fifteenth century. It is a timber-framed hall house and has been heavily restored. Next to it, where the main college once stood, is a delightful farmhouse described by Nikolaus Pevsner as 'one of the best in Surrey'. The brick building was erected about 1700 and has a fine Horsham slate roof and original windows. The front is tile hung, a feature which was restored in the nineteenth century.

The church itself is a rarity in Surrey in that it is the county's only Perpendicular church of note which has not been over-restored. Outstanding late medieval fittings and monuments make it a great pleasure to explore inside and because of these it has been dubbed the 'Westminster Abbey of Surrey'. The lectern is fifteenth century as are the screens between the chancel and the north and south chapels. The fifteenth-century stalls are beautifully carved.

Of the monuments, and there are many tombs and brasses, those dedicated to the Cobham family are the most impressive. Sir Reginald Cobham, who died in 1446 fifteen years after he rebuilt the church, and his wife lie in a grand chest tomb with alabaster effigies of them both on the top. His head rests on the helmet of a Moor's head, and his feet on a sea wolf and a dragon. These carvings are exceptionally expressive. The 1st Baron Cobham who accompanied the Black Prince at Crécy, died of plague in 1361 and was buried in the north chapel in another impressive tomb chest. His head rests on the head of a Saracen which indicated that he was

descended from a crusader. On top of the tomb of
the 2nd Baron, who died in 1403, is a fine brass. The
unmarked tomb next to this is believed to be that of
Sir Thomas Cobham, who died in 1471, and his wife
Anne, a descendant of Edward III.

The brasses in the church are regarded as the best
in Surrey. They include figures of priests and
fifteenth-century ladies. One of these is particularly
outstanding. It is believed to be of Elizabeth, second
wife of Sir Reginald Cobham, shown in full-size with
intricately draped clothing and a pet dog at her feet.
Also in the church are two fine wall monuments to
Francis Howard, who died in 1695, and his wife
Mary who lived until 1718. The Royal Arms of
Queen Anne are carved on the north wall of the
nave.

Other historic buildings in the village include
some delightful tile-hung and timber-framed cottages
dating from the fifteenth and sixteenth centuries,
many of them in the main street. New Place is a
lovely Wealden stone house built in 1617. An
unusual building in the village centre by its pretty
duckpond is **St Peter's Cross and Cage** (Other
Historic Buildings). The Cross is believed to date
from the fifteenth century and the cage was added in
1773. It is a tiny lockup, last used to hold a poacher
in 1882, with a little turret and stone roof.

Mickleham   Map 4 Aa

Mickleham lies in the most beautiful stretch of the
Mole valley with Box Hill rising above it. The area
has been dubbed 'Little Switzerland' because of its
lovely wooded hills and deep valley below.

At the foot of **Box Hill** (Country Parks) is
Juniper Hall (Field Study) owned by the National
Trust and used as a field study centre for this area of
rich natural life, abundant in rare butterflies and
plants. It was built in the late eighteenth century.

O

Nearby is Flint Cottage, the home of George Meredith, the novelist, from 1867 until his death in 1907. Here he wrote *Diana of the Crossways* working in a chalet he built on the steep slope of his garden. Fanny Burney also has connections with the area. She met her husband, General D'Arblay, at Juniper Hall in 1793 when he had sought refuge there during the French Revolution. They later married in Mickleham church and returned to live in West Humble in 1797 in Camilla Cottage, which has since been destroyed, until D'Arblay was able to return to France in 1802.

The Norman tower of the church of St Michael stands high above the village. There are other Norman features including a twelfth-century font. The beautifully carved pulpit is late fifteenth century and came from Belgium and the west window contains sixteenth-century Flemish stained-glass. In the graveyard are some rare old wooden grave-boards which have been carefully preserved. Close to the church in the village is Old House, built in 1636 but altered in the eighteenth century. The Running Horses Inn is seventeenth century and there are some delightful old cottages.

Marie Stopes, an early twentieth-century pioneer of birth control, lived near the village at Norbury Park, an eighteenth-century mansion.

Ockham Map 1 Bc

This attractive village has many Victorian buildings including pretty cottages. Ockham Park was the local manor with a fine house built in the early fifteenth century for Henry Weston. Sadly it was mostly destroyed by fire in 1948. In its landscaped grounds stands All Saints church, built mainly in the thirteenth century with an outstanding east window, also thirteenth-century, and intricately carved capitals. It is extremely rare to find such fine details from the Early English period of architecture. There are also some good brasses and monuments in the church. A brass memorial to Walter Frilende, dated 1376, is the oldest priest's brass in the county. The best monument is by the sculptor Rysbrack to the first Lord King who died in 1734.

Ockham Mill is a five-storey brick building erected in 1862. The Hautboy Hotel is strong Victorian Gothic, built in 1864.

Ockley Map 4 Ba

This lovely old village has stood on the main route from London to Chichester for centuries. It was an important smuggling route and the villains involved probably used the old inns here, some of which survive.

The village's pride and joy is its magnificent green, up to 600 feet wide and the setting for cricket throughout the summer in traditional Surrey style.

All Saints Church

There are also some fine old buildings: tile-hung and timber-framed cottages, a classic Georgian brick house and Tuns House, a very pretty eighteenth-century weatherboarded house. The church is unusual for such a village in that it does not stand on the green but at what must once have been the centre, half a mile northeast where a castle once stood. St Margaret's was largely rebuilt in 1873 but has kept its fifteenth-century wooden porch.

Leith Hill (Country Parks) provides a lovely backdrop to the village, reaching over 950 feet, the highest point in Surrey and southeast England. The slopes of Leith Hill where the Saxons once defeated marauding Danes in A.D. 851, are covered in pine woodland, much of it protected by the National Trust. On its summit is a folly tower which can be climbed, taking the visitor over 1,000 feet above sea level. Spectacular views can be enjoyed, with the English Channel often visible. The tower was first built by Richard Hull in 1766 and he is buried beneath it. Legend says that after his death the smugglers used it to hide their loot. The tower was heightened in 1788 and then given Victorian Gothic battlements and a turret in 1864.

Richard Hull lived at **Leith Hill Place** whose gardens are open all year, a grand house in a superb position on the south slope of the hill. Here also lived the Wedgewood family for many years and the house contains a large collection of their famous pottery as well as portraits of the family. It was also owned at a later date by Vaughan Williams the composer. The house was given its stone-facing in the mid-eighteenth century but the body of the building dates back to about 1600.

Petersham Map 3 Aa

Close to Richmond, and now part of Greater London, is this grand village of grand houses. Close to London, yet neighbouring the Royal hunting parks and pleasure gardens of Richmond and Kew, and situated on the banks of the Thames, this became a desirable residential area as early as the seventeenth century. Sadly twentieth-century traffic congestion now suffocates the place and it is hard to see the lovely mansions lying close together at the village centre.

Petersham House is late seventeenth-century but its delightful domed porch with Ionic columns dates from the first years of the nineteenth century. Rutland Lodge was built in 1666 for the Lord Mayor of London. It was enlarged in about 1720 and like its neighbour has a fine entrance with Doric columns. It stands at the end of River Lane, which leads down to the Thames, and contains Petersham Lodge. Built in the mid-eighteenth century with a rotunda in the garden, it was used by John Gay, the eighteenth-century dramatist and poet who lived nearby in Richmond but often stayed at the house. Also in River Lane is the early eighteenth-century Manor House.

In Sudbrook Lane more outstanding houses, including Gort Lodge and Harrington Lodge, lead down to the golf club which occupies the grounds of one of the grandest houses in the area, Sudbrook Park. The Duke of Argyll built his home here in 1726, a classical brick building. The Old House in Hazel Lane was originally erected, in 1487, at Cuxton in Kent and owned by another Lord Mayor of London. In 1925 it was reconstructed here.

Petersham's parish church of St Peter is well worth visiting. Parts date from the thirteenth century with extensive eighteenth and nineteenth-century rebuilding, but carried out without disturbing the charm of the church. The interior has been well-preserved. It has eighteenth-century woodwork, including box pews, a fine pulpit and a gallery. An unusual and colourful monument shows three figures, a man, his wife and their grandson, lying on their sides but looking very much alive and alert. He was George Cole who died in 1624.

The main road through Petersham leads down to the old village of Ham. **Ham House** (Historic Homes), however, is much closer to Petersham. It is one of the finest stately homes close to London. The writer Horace Walpole said of it in 1770 that 'Close to the Thames, in the centre of rich and verdant beauty, it is so blocked up and barricaded with walls, vast trees, and gates that you think yourself an hundred miles off and an hundred years back'. Ham House was first built by Sir Thomas Vavasour in 1610 during the Stuart period and slightly altered in the eighteenth century. In the 1670s it was redecorated by Vavasour's daughter and her husband, the Duke and Duchess of Lauderdale and it is the resulting splendour of the baroque decorations that most visitors come to see. There is a vast Great Hall hung with fine paintings, including works by Kneller, Hoppner and Reynold, and a superb plaster ceiling, unusually progressive in its design and detail for that period; a marble dining room with gilt-leather hangings; the Duchess's stately bedchamber with four sea paintings by Van de Velde; and a small chapel with the original fittings. The sweeping walnut staircase, rebuilt in 1638, is intricately carved and leads to more grand rooms, many with good plasterwork and containing more art treasures including fine tapestries and paintings, and many examples of the original seventeenth-century furniture. The house is owned by the Department of the Environment but administered by the Victoria and Albert Museum.

Ham village was another desirable residential area close to London and has lovely commons faced by seventeenth- and eighteenth-century houses.

Puttenham   Map 2 Ab

The Hog's Back ridge carries an ancient road,
forming part of the Pilgrim's Way, from Guildford to
Farnham along one of the most scenic routes in
southern England. It passes through many lovely
villages of which Puttenham is perhaps the most
picturesque. The village straddles the road forming a
pretty line of old buildings along the ridge with
views across delightful pastoral land on either side.

St John the Baptist church was restored by Henry
Woodyer in 1861 but not without adding some new
character to the basic twelfth-century building.
Inside it is particularly attractive with a four-bay
arcade dating from about 1160 and a slightly later
chancel arch. The north chapel was partially rebuilt
in 1770 and the tower, although largely rebuilt
during restoration, was originally fifteenth century.
There is a priest's brass of the early fifteenth century
and in the graveyard lies Esther Bellasis, said to
have died of a broken heart in 1805 when her
husband George was transported to Botany Bay in
Australia after killing a man in a duel.

Close to the church is Puttenham Priory, a fine
Palladian house with a striking entrance built in
1762. The other lovely building by the church is
Greys Home Farm, with its weatherboarded barns
and oasthouses, dating from the eighteenth century.
Two leading Victorian architects worked in the
village. The Tudor-style Rectory designed by John
Perry and Hurlands was the last country house built
by Philip Webb. The village's cottages are a
harmonious mixture of sandstone and brick with
half-timbering and tile-hanging.

Redhill   Map 4 Ab

Until the early nineteenth century this was open
country. The town developed because of its situation

R

on the main route from London to Brighton so it has a certain Victorian harmony and character all of its own. In 1807 a road was built to the new coastal resort and in 1841 the railway was opened here in Redhill, alongside the road. Redhill later became a junction for the railways with a line going east to Tonbridge and west to Guildford.

It is now a part of the suburban sprawl which also takes in its medieval neighbour, Reigate, but some of the impressive Victorian buildings, erected as the town was established, remain. St John's church stands on the common and was built first in 1867 and altered between 1889-95 to give it a spacious nave and a handsome southwest tower and spire. The town soon became popular with businessmen who worked in London but wanted to live outside the metropolis and some of their impressive homes survive. These include The Firs, on the Brighton road south of the centre, built in about 1830 in the Regency-style. The Market Hall which once overlooked a thriving market place was built in the Jacobean style in 1860.

Reigate Map 4 Ab

Only fragments of the history of this ancient town can be appreciated today since it has become a popular residential centre for commuters. William the Conqueror gave the manor and seat here, already in existence as a settlement, to the Earl of Surrey, de Warenne, who fortified the estate with a strong castle. In Castle Grounds the mound on which it stood can still be seen though nothing else remains. The gateway to Castle Grounds is medieval in style but dates from the eighteenth century.

Of the many old buildings which stand overwhelmed by modern development, two are outstanding: the parish church and Reigate Priory. The church of St Mary Magdalene stands on a hill

and is an impressively large building. Its oldest
section is the nave, dating from the late twelfth
century, with fine arcades. There are several
seventeenth- and eighteenth-century monuments
including a fine one of Richard Ladbroke who died
in 1730. The vestry holds a library founded by the
vicar in 1701 and contains a wide-ranging collection
of theological books. In the vault of the church lies
Lord Howard of Effingham who led the English fleet
against the Spanish Armada and died in 1624.

Lord Howard of Effingham was given Reigate
Priory by Henry VIII after the Dissolution in 1541.
The priory had been founded in 1235 for
Augustinian canons and Effingham replaced the old
building with a fine Tudor manor. Little of this
remains for the house was again rebuilt in 1776. The
interior contains two outstanding features: a
magnificent fireplace in the hall and an unusual and
beautiful painted staircase. The fireplace is the
subject of some controversy since it is claimed to
be the work of Holbein. When John Evelyn saw the
stone fireplace's massive carved timber overmantel
and surround in 1655, he claimed that it was by
Holbein and had been moved from Katherine Parr's
home at Bletchingley which was later owned by the
Howards. The eighteenth-century staircase is also
beautifully carved and the stairwell has paintings
showing classical scenes attributed to the Italian
artist Verrio. The whole was carefully conceived to
provide a lovely harmonious centre to the house as
one climbs up to the landings. Pevsner describes it as
one of the best staircases in England.

The attractive Old Town Hall which dominates
Reigate's centre was built in 1728. An interesting
feature of the town is its medieval underground cave
system, known as Baron's Cave because it is believed
that the Barons met here before singing the Magna
Carta. They lie below the castle mound in Castle

R

Grounds and originally stretched, it is said, as far as
Bletchingley Castle. In 1824 a new section of road
tunnel was cut through to provide an unusual
approach to the town.

Richmond Map 3 Aa

Richmond is undoubtedly one of the treasures of
Surrey, now enveloped by London but still retaining
its own character, charm and grandeur. The superb
Green was the setting for jousting tournaments in
the fourteenth century. Overlooking it was a royal
palace enjoyed by monarchs for centuries. From the
lovely Terrace Gardens one can enjoy another
important Richmond feature, the view down the
Thames, as magnificent today as when Turner
painted it. Looking across at extensive woodland and
green hills it is difficult to believe that London is so
close by. Perhaps the town is most well known for
the vast expanse of Richmond Park, a favourite
hunting ground for monarchs from the seventeenth
century. Today its herds of deer have a more
peaceful life and thousands of visitors enjoy the park
each year.

Royal Richmond started when Edward III built a
palace in a village then called Sheen. East Sheen still
exists nearby. The village name referred to the
shining river Thames beside which it stood. Sheen
Palace where he died in 1377 was his favourite
residence. Henry V extended the palace using
materials from Byfleet Manor but his creation was
destroyed by fire in 1499. Henry VII then erected a
grand Tudor mansion which he called Richmond
Palace and the village soon adopted this name.
Henry VIII used it a great deal and eventually gave
it to Anne of Cleves. Elizabeth I was born beside the
Thames and died at Richmond in 1603, in the palace
which had been her favourite home. It was used by
Henry Prince of Wales and Charles Prince of Wales,

later Charles I, before it lost favour with the Royal Family and was sold in decay in 1649. Today only the brick gatehouse survives bearing the arms of Henry VII.

However the Green is overlooked by some superb old buildings. On the southwest side is Maids of Honour Row, built in 1724 to house Caroline Princess of Wales' maids of honour. The terrace has three-storey houses with five-bay fronts, approached through iron gates and railings. Wardrobe Court adjoins the remains of the old palace gatehouse on Old Palace Yard and is early eighteenth century with Tudor brickwork incorporated from the palace of Henry VII. Another outstanding building on the Green is Trumpeter's House, built at the beginning of the eighteenth century with a grand portico entrance flanked by two pairs of Tuscan columns.

Between the Green and the riverside are lovely narrow streets of old houses and pretty cottages. The

The Thames, Richmond

R

parish church of St Mary Magdalene, however, is now cut off from its original village surrounds by large industrial and commercial buildings. The church's fifteenth-century stone tower is its oldest fragment, largely rebuilt in 1624, whilst the body of the church dates from about 1750. Inside, the font and pulpit are both eighteenth century and there are several seventeenth- and eighteenth-century monuments. A notable one from the nineteenth century is to Edmund Kean, the actor, who lived on the Green and appeared at the Richmond theatre which stood on the site overlooking the Green, now occupied by Garrick House.

Richmond Bridge's stone arches were created by James Paine in 1777. Across from Bridge Street is Ormond Road with its fine Georgian buildings. The Vineyard runs parallel to this and contains two old almshouse groups. Bishop Duppa's Almshouses were founded in 1661 and rebuilt in 1850 and Queen Elizabeth's Almshouses date from 1767, but on the site of an earlier group. Nearby is another set, Michel's Almshouses, founded in 1659 and rebuilt in 1811.

Leading off from The Vineyard is Richmond Hill with more fine houses and the delightful Terrace Gardens, created in 1887 as the gardens for Buccleugh House. Following Richmond Hill towards Richmond Park are two exceptional Georgian houses. The Wick was built in 1775 and beside it is Wick House, built for Sir Joshua Reynolds, the artist, in 1772. It's position offers a lovely view of the Thames which Reynolds painted.

Richmond Park is the largest enclosed space in Greater London and is over 2,000 acres in size. The eleven-mile wall which encloses this beautiful parkland was completed for Charles I in 1637. The area was then stocked with deer and royal hunting parties pursued them for sport until well into the eighteenth century. Private shooting was allowed in the park until as late as 1904. But today it is a haven of peace and tranquillity, spoilt only by the traffic which can be easily escaped on foot. Herds of deer, fallow deer and red deer, still roam the park which includes wide expanses of bracken, woodland and common, also an area of ponds and a golf course. The Isabella Plantation is a delightful section of paths and streams surrounded by magnificent flowering shrubs and rare trees, particularly impressive and colourful in early summer.

White Lodge was begun in 1728 for George I but completed later as a hunting lodge for George II. The grand ashlar house was the birthplace of the Duke of Windsor and now houses the Royal Ballet School. Another fine house in the park is Thatched House Lodge, built for Sir Robert Walpole from 1727. It has a smaller summer house, Thatched House, in its gardens. Pembroke Lodge is another eighteenth century building.

Richmond has important literary associations as well as its royal patrons and links with artists and actors. The poet, James Thompson, is buried in the parish church and he lived from 1736 until his death in 1748 at a cottage in Kew Foot Lane. In 1744 he published *The Seasons* a series of poems which include references to the area. Several of Charles Dickens' books also contain scenes set in Richmond, for he was fond of the district and knew it well. He stayed here first in 1836 for a holiday and returned in 1839 to rent Elm Cottage (now Elm Lodge) in Petersham Road. He was also a frequent visitor to the Star and Garter Hotel, which he used as a venue for celebrations such as the publication of a new novel or the birth of his son. Marian (Mary Ann) Evans first used her pseudonym, George Eliot, for her novel *Amos Barton* which she wrote from her

R

home at 8 Park Shot, now The Courthouse. She also started *Adam Bede* here before moving in 1859. The Hogarth Press was named by its founders, Virginia and Leonard Woolf, after Hogarth House on Paradise Road. They lived there from 1915-1924 after living on The Green in 1914.

Runnymede   Map 1 Ab

The meadows of Runnymede contain the historic site where King John signed the Magna Carta on 15 June 1215. After a long struggle between the King and his barons the two factions stood on either side of the Thames. The King waited at Windsor Castle while the barons, who had taken London, marched to Staines and crossed the Thames before setting up camp on the fields of Runnymede. The King met their leaders here for long negotiations which resulted in the signing of the charter and ended the supreme rule of the monarchy in England. The memorial which marks the exact spot where the signing took place was raised in 1957 by the American Bar Association with the inscription 'To commemorate Magna Carta, symbol of freedom under law'.

Nearby is another important memorial to John F. Kennedy, the American president who was assasinated in 1963. The inscription contains part of his inauguration speech which referred to the Magna Carta. A third memorial in the area is to the Commonwealth Air Forces who fought during the Second World War.

The National Trust now administer **Runnymede Country Park** whose 200 acres of lovely pastureland contain these memorials on Cooper's Hill. The gatehouses at the entrance were designed by Edwin Lutyens and one contains a tearoom. Boat trips can be enjoyed down the Thames from the park which once contained the Egham racecourse, a fashionable setting for horse-racing from the eighteenth century until 1886. It closed in that year because the local police no longer agreed to supply a force to keep order at the meetings.

Shalford see Guildford

Sheen see Richmond

Shere Map 2 Ac

This picturesque village is perhaps most pretty at Church Square, where the High Street with its gabled houses can be best appreciated. The Norman church of St James has a thirteenth-century tower and spire, finely restored this century. A Norman arch forms the entrance with zigzag decoration and on entering the church the full extent of the interior can be enjoyed, leading down to a rare fourteenth-century east window containing fragments of its

Shere

S

original stained glass. The font is also from that period, as is a Crusader Chest originally used to collect money to finance Christian knights. Two fifteenth century brasses commemorate Robert Scarcliffe, Rector of Shere, who died in 1412, and John Lord Audley who died in 1491. In the north wall of the chancel is a tiny cell built in 1329 to hold Christine, the daughter of William the Carpenter. Legend relates that she chose to be incarcerated, but that she escaped some years later, was recaptured and returned to her cramped prison. Through a squint hole she could see the altar and she received sacrament through a small window. The lynchgate to the church was designed by Edwin Lutyens in 1901.

Lutyens did much work to make this village lovely. He built the gate lodge to the nineteenth-century Shere Manor House and a pair of cottages nearby. In the High Street is a half-timbered shop front by him. Lower Street which runs off Church Square contains Ash Cottage and dates from about 1600. Beyond this is the Old Prison House, a seventeenth-century half-timbered building. There are also early seventeenth-century half-timbered buildings in the High Street.

Beside the stream which runs through the village is an old cornmill, now a pumping station. This stream provided water for the abundance of watercress beds which are still a feature of Shere.

Stoke D'Abernon Map 3 Ba

This village is now engulfed by the suburban sprawl but has two outstanding buildings, its church and manor house. The brasses in St Mary's church include the oldest in England. The brass effigy commemorates Sir John D'Abernon who died in 1277. The Knight stands in full armour carrying a shield which is enamelled in blue. The brass is six feet six inches long. Another brass to his son, also Sir John, who died in 1327, stands beside it. Two fifteenth-century brasses can also be seen. Anne Norbury, who died in 1469, is shown with her eight children in the folds of her dress.

Roman bricks were used when the church was first built in Saxon times, as early as the seventh century. The north aisle was added in the early twelfth century and more additions and restorations were made over the centuries. The Jacobean pulpit was presented to the church in 1620 and there are fragments of the thirteenth-century wall painting in the chancel. The fifteenth-century stained glass was installed this century and came from Costessey Hall in Norfolk. The D'Abernon and Vincent families' heraldic shields can be seen in the Norbury Chapel which was built in 1490.

The church stands beside the pretty river Mole

Thursley

T

and is approached down an avenue of chestnuts which also leads to the Manor House, in a lovely situation on the river banks. Sections of the original sixteenth-century building remain but it dates mainly from 1757. It was built first for the Vincent family who have several fine memorials in the church.

Tilford see Farnham

Thorpe see Chertsey

Thursley Map 2 Bb

The name Thursley means 'field of Thor', the northern god of war given to the settlement by its Saxon occupants. They built a church here which has been sadly over-restored but retains fragments of the original. The wooden belfry and spire are fifteenth century as is the stained glass in the north aisle which, as at Stoke D'Abernon, was bought this century from Norfolk.

In medieval times the village was a thriving centre for the iron and glass industries and this conservation area is well-preserved with many charming old cottages and houses surrounded by mature trees. The Parsonage, Wheeler's Farm and Old Hall each date from the sixteenth century. The poet John Freeman, who died in 1929, is buried in the churchyard. Also buried here is the unfortunate sailor whose murder in 1786 gave Gibbets Hill, nearby, its name after his three assassins were hanged there.

Thursley is the birthplace, in 1869, of one of Surrey's most distinguished sons, the architect Edwin Lutyens. In his early days he lived at what is now called Lutyens House and when only 19 he converted a row of cottages in the village to form the house, The Corner. A flowering shrub on the village green was planted in memory of a legendary Sussex personality William Cobbet who wrote *Rural Rides*. The long distance pathway, **The Greensand Way** (Walking) follows the Ridge via Thursley, from Haslemere to Hascombe.

Virginia Water   Map 1 Ab

This is one of the most expensive and attractive suburban areas of Surrey, known for its magnificent leafy avenues and for the section of **Windsor Great Park** (Country Parks) which it encloses. The lake

The Cascade

W

here is a famous beauty spot with an expanse of water over 160 acres in size. The Virginia Water lake was created by Thomas and Paul Sandby when they landscaped the park for the Duke of Cumberland between 1746-1768. The Duke was known as 'the butcher' after his victory at the Battle of Culloden. Boating can be enjoyed on the lake and there are many beautifully sited picnic spots around it. Long walks can be enjoyed through the park. **Valley Gardens** within the park cover 300 acres, containing glorious rhododendrons, camellias, magnolias and various shrubs.

In the centre of Virginia Water is the Holloway Sanatorium which, like Royal Holloway College, was built by the wealthy philanthropist and pill manufacturer Thomas Holloway and designed by his architect W.H. Crossland. Between here and Sunningdale, another leafy suburb, is Fort Belvedere, a favourite home of the Duke of Windsor when he was Prince of Wales and Edward VIII, between 1930 and his abdication in 1939. It was built for the Duke of Cumberland in 1750 and converted for George IV in 1828.

Walton-on-the-Hill Map 4 Ab

Situated on the Downs to the south of Epsom is this attractive village which marks the site of an ancient settlement. The Romans built two villas nearby and the village was first settled by Saxons. It then became an important manor during Norman times. The fourteenth-century manor house no longer stands but sections of the walls and other fragments in the late nineteenth century Walton Manor are from this original building.

The church of St Peter was originally Norman but the building has a fifteenth-century chancel and other notable Perpendicular features. It was restored in the nineteenth century. Inside is the oldest lead font in England, dating from about 1150. The moulded frieze is a rare example of Romanesque sculpture consisting of finely shaped leaf motifs and eight figures seated under arches. It is believed that the decoration was first designed to include twelve figures and arches, representing the twelve Apostles, but was cut down to make eight. Some sections of the church's stained glass are sixteenth- century Flemish glass brought from Woburn Abbey.

The famous Epsom Races were originally staged here on the Walton Downs and racing stables still survive in the surrounding valleys. The village is now best known in the sporting world for its excellent golf course.

Wanborough   Map 2 Ab

Wanborough is an exceptionally attractive group of buildings forming a tiny hamlet which has long historic associations. It is believed that the first settlers here discovered the spring 10,000 years ago and a Bronze Age burial mound was visible until earlier this century when it was flattened during road building. The Saxons called the hamlet Wenberge which means 'bump barrow', presumably referring to the mound. The little thirteenth-century church is just one tiny room on the site of a Saxon chapel mentioned in the Domesday Book. The church was built by the monks of Waverley Abbey in Farnham who acquired the manor here in 1130. Roman tiles were used in the walls which are mainly flint and rubble and the west wall was rebuilt in the seventeenth century when the church was used for secular purposes. It was restored in 1862.

The monks also built the beautiful barn with its fine king-beam roof. They used it originally to store wool and it later became a tithe barn. Wanborough Manor is seventeenth century, though a house was built here in 1527. In the late nineteenth century it was the home of Sir Algernon West, private secretary to Gladstone, and Queen Victoria was one of his distinguished visitors. During the Second World War it was a secret centre for the allies' intelligence organization, the Special Operations Executive, and spies and saboteurs were trained there before being sent behind enemy lines.

West Clandon   see East Clandon

West Horsley   see Horsley

Weybridge   Map 1 Bc

The medieval village here became popular with royalty in Tudor times when Henry VIII had two grand homes, Oatlands Park, which he built in 1588, and Ashley Park, both long gone. Today it is the centre of Surrey's 'gin and tonic' belt of grand suburban homes in the districts of Oatlands, once the estate of Henry VIII's mansion, and St George's Hill, now famous for its exclusive golf club. The hotel at Oatlands was originally a hunting lodge built by Henry Holland in 1794 which became a private house in 1827 and was converted to a hotel in 1856.

The medieval church of St James was rebuilt in 1855 but the pleasant interior contains ancient brasses and some fine memorials. In Thames Street are two Tudor fragments, a garden wall and an arch. The Ship Hotel which faces Monument Green in the High Street is seventeenth century. The green is so-named because of the fine monument to the Duchess of York, who lived at Oatlands Park. The column and pedestal stood at London's Seven Dials until 1773 and were created in 1694. They were re-erected here in 1822.

Weybridge Museum has displays on the history of northwest Surrey including archaeology, local history, folk byegones, handicrafts and costumes.

Whiteley Village   Map 3 Ba

When he died in 1907, William Whiteley, the wealthy owner of a Bayswater store, left a million pounds to be used to build a village for 'thrifty old people'. 225 acres of Surrey countryside were purchased in 1911 and after a competition Frank Atkinson was chosen as the architect to execute Whiteley's desire. He in turn commissioned other architects to assist and the village was created between 1914 and 1921.

Unlike Hampstead Garden Suburb, started in 1907, Atkinson did not try and create a pretty village atmosphere but opted for neat formality. He chose to use classic architectural styles rather than Hampstead's mock-Gothic design and set the buildings in beautifully landscaped surrounds. There is one building in the medieval style, St Mark's church which is based on thirteenth century design. Chestnut Walk is the hub of activity with its shops and communal kitchen, chapels and a village club and hall.

Wisley   Map 1 Bc

The old buildings of the church and adjoining church farm are to the north of the small village beside the River Wey. The Norman twelfth-century church has been heavily restored and has an attractive seventeenth-century porch and windows. The farmhouse is L-shaped and half-timbered sections date from the sixteenth century with the brick infilling dating from the eighteenth century.

The village is dominated by the Royal Horticultural Society's **Wisley Gardens**. These experimental gardens and laboratories were housed at Chiswick until 1904 when 60 acres of land here was presented to the society as a gift. Wisley Gardens now cover over 300 acres including farm and woodland. All aspects of gardening are covered in a series of different plantings. There is a magnificent display of ornamental plants; fruit and vegetable gardens; specialist gardens such as herbs, heather, roses and wild plants; glasshouses and trial grounds for experiments with rare and unusual plants; and areas of shrubs and trees. An important feature is the garden for the disabled, created to encourage gardening for the disabled. The whole of the gardens are easily accessible by wheelchair.

The purpose of the Wisley Gardens is to carry out horticultural and botanical experiments and to offer advice and service to members of the Royal Horticultural Society. Anyone who enjoys gardens will appreciate the lovely displays, particularly in spring and autumn, whilst keen gardeners will find inspiration and ideas. Gardening demonstrations are given at stated times throughout the year.

Woking   Map 1 Bc

This Victorian town developed with the advent of the railway from the late 1830s and has grown into one of Surrey's largest towns. Amid its nineteenth and twentieth-century buildings is a major centre for the Islamic religion in Britain. The Shah Jehan Mosque was founded in 1885 by Dr Gottlieb Leitner in a former drama college. He was a linguist and Orientalist creating a centre for Islamic studies. In 1869 the new mosque was built in Indian style.

Two miles from the centre of Woking is Old Woking, the original settlement which dates back to Saxon times when, as the Domesday Book recalls, it was owned by the king. It was a market town in the seventeenth century and has many fine old buildings. The church of St Peter is originally Norman with a thirteenth-century chancel and seventeenth-century pulpit and gallery. Norman remnants include the lovely Romanesque doorway. Inside are some fine old monuments and brasses.

The main street of the old town contains a seventeenth-century Manor House and an eighteenth-century building now divided into two, forming Magnolia and Old Brew House. North of the town lies Hoe Place, a seventeenth-century house altered in the eighteenth century when it was given a Regency front. Further east are the ruins of Woking Old Hall, once a grand, though small, Tudor royal palace given by James I to Edward Zouch who abandoned it for his new home at Hoe Place. It is a damp moated site with only foundations to be seen. An early house stands nearby, Woking Park Farm, which was altered at the beginning of the seventeenth century.

Surrey Route Map

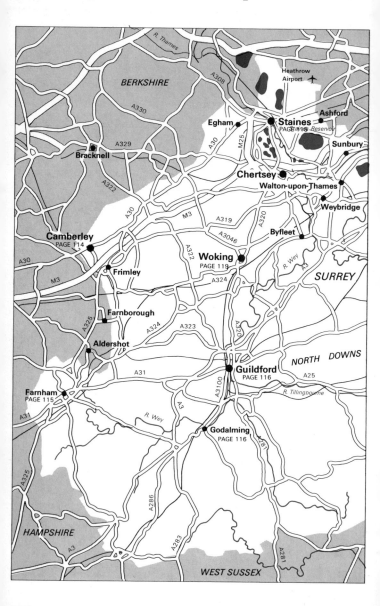

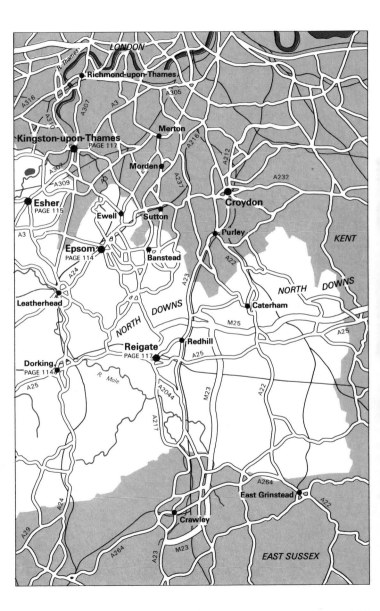

LONDON

Richmond-upon-Thames

A316
A307
A3
A305
A305
A310

Kingston-upon-Thames
PAGE 117

Merton

A217

A212

A232

Esher
PAGE 115

A301
A309
A3

Ewell

Morden

A237

Croydon

KENT

A3

Sutton

Epsom
PAGE 114

Banstead

Purley

A24

A23

A22

NORTH DOWNS

Leatherhead

NORTH DOWNS

Caterham

M25

A25

Reigate
PAGE 117

Redhill

A25

Dorking
PAGE 114

R. Mole

A2044

M23

A22

A25

A24

A217

A29

A264

A23

M23

Crawley

East Grinstead

A264

A22

EAST SUSSEX

109

Map 1

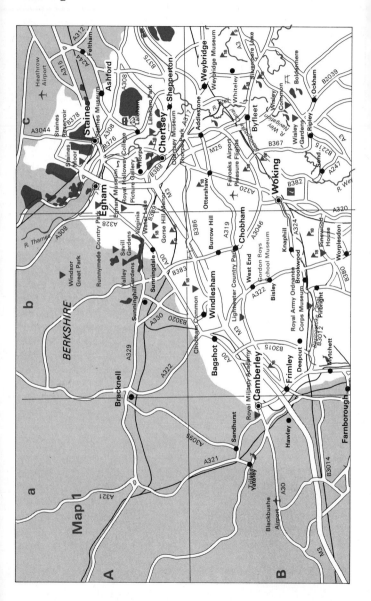

Map 2

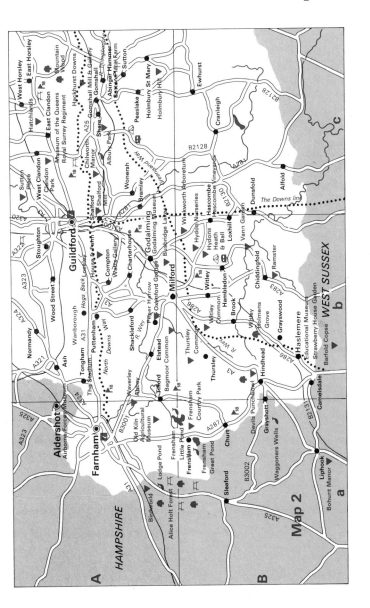

Map 3

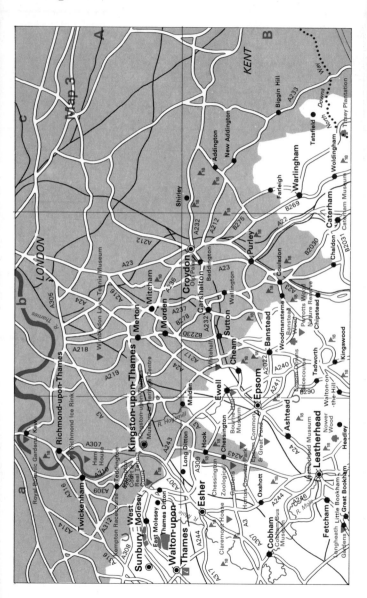

Map 4

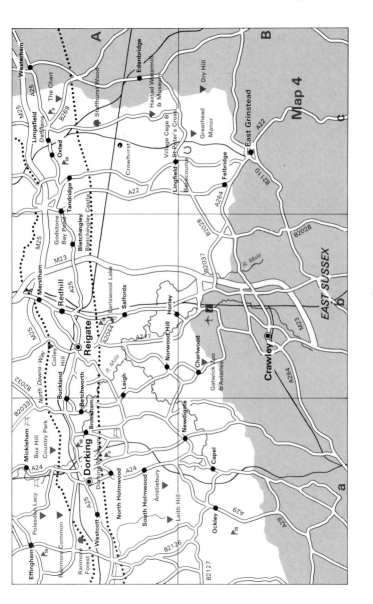

Town Directory

Camberley
Map 1 Ba

Museum: Royal Military Academy Sandhurst Collection
Nearby:
Country Park: Lightwater Country Park
Museum: Royal Army Corps Museum

Dorking
Map 4 Aa

Museum: Dorking Museum
Crafts: The Craft Shop
Market: See Markets
Nearby:
Art Gallery: Gomshall Mill & Art Gallery
Country Parks: Box Hill, Ranmore Common
Garden: Sutton Place Farm
Historic Home: Polesden Lacey
Nature Reserve: Hackhurst Downs
Woodlands: Ranmore Forest, Mountain

Epsom & Ewell
Map 3 Ba

Country Parks: Epsom Common, Horton Country Park
Horseracing: Epsom Downs Racecourse
Market: See Markets
Museum: Bourne Hall Museum
Other Historic Building: Whitehall

Esher
Map 3 Ba

Garden: Claremont Landscape Garden
Historic Home: Claremont
Horseracing: Sandown Racecourse
Nearby:
Country Park: Horton Country Park
Zoo: Chessington Zoological Gardens

Farnham
Map 2 Aa

Castle: Farnham Castle
Museum: Farnham Museum
Sports Centre: Farnham Sports Centre
Nearby:
Church Buildings: Waverley Abbey
Country Park: Frensham Country Park
Crafts: New Ashgate Gallery, Ridgeway House Farm
Motor Racing: The Stadium
Museums: Airborne Forces Museum, Old Kiln Agricultural
Woodland: Alice Holt Forest
Zoos: Birdworld

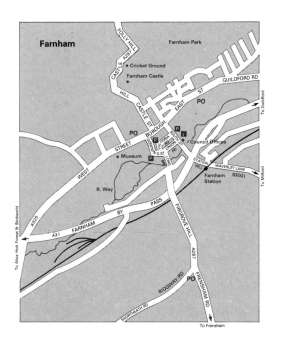

Godalming
Map 2 Ab

🚍 ∪ ⅔ ⚓ ♪

Market: See Markets
Museum: Godalming Museum
Nearby:
Bird Park: Busbridge Lakes
Gardens: Hydon Nurseries,
Winkworth Arboretum
Nature Reserves: Bagmoor
Common, Witley Common
Other Historic Buildings:
Oxenford Grange
Vineyard: Hascombe Vineyard

Guildford
Map 2 Ab

ⅈ₁₈ 🛈 ∪ ⅔ ⚓ ♪

Art Gallery: Guildford House
Gallery

Castle: Guildford Castle
Church Buildings: Hospital of
the Blessed Trinity, Guildford
Cathedral, Bishop's Palace
Crafts: Jim Fox Gold & Silver
Designs
Markets: See Markets
Museums: Brooking Collection,
Guildford Museum, Women's
Royal Army Corps Museum
Sports Centre: Guildford
Sports Centre
Nearby:
Art Gallery: Sutton Place
Farm: Loseley House & Farm
Garden: Chilworth Manor
Historic Homes: Albury Park,
Clandon Park, Hatchlands
Mill: Shalford Mill
Museum: Museum of the
Queen's Royal Surrey Regiment

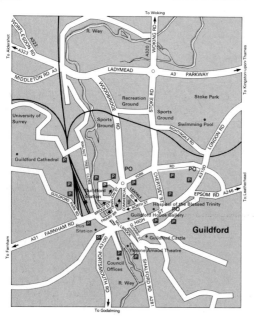

Kingston-upon-Thames
Map 3 Aa

⛵ 🎵

Historic Home: Hampton Court
Museum: Kingston Museum & Heritage Centre
Nearby:
Historic Home: Ham House
Horseracing: Kempton Racecourse

Reigate
Map 4 Ab

🏔 U 🎣 ⛵ 🎵

Market: See Markets
Mills: Reigate Heath Windmill, Wray Common Windmill
Nearby:
Castle: Bletchingley Castle
Country Park: Colley Hill

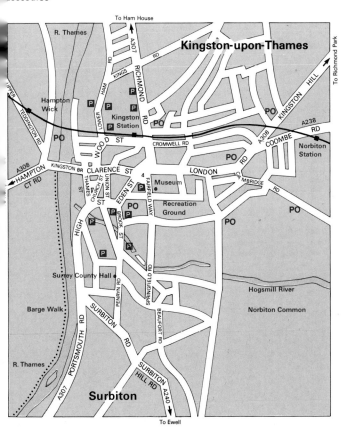

Staines
Map 1 Ac

Birdwatching: Staines
Reservoir
Museum: Staines Museum
Nature Reserve: Staines Moor
Sports Centre: Staines Sports
Centre
Nearby:
Art Gallery: Royal Holloway
College Picture Gallery
Country Park: Runnymede
Country Park
Gardens: Savill Gardens, Gorse
Hill Manor
Museum: Egham Museum

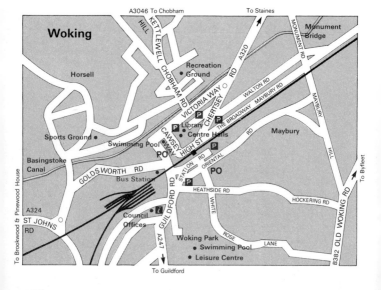

Woking
Map 1 Bc

Market: See Markets
Museum: Gordon Boy's School
Museum
Sports Centre: Woking Leisure
Centre
Nearby:
Gardens: Wisley Gardens,
Pinewood House

Leisure A-Z

Details given here have been carefully checked but are subject to change. Last admission can be half an hour before stated closing time.

Symbols: See p 5.

Abbreviations: ch children

ch16	children to age 16
m	mile
N	north
S	south
E	east
W	west

Aerobics

Aerobics is an energetic form of keep fit developed in the United States. At present there is no governing body for aerobics in this country and no central source of information for classes. Some sports centres are planning aerobics classes and local council Adult Education Centres will be doing them. Contact your local sports centre or council for details. In Surrey Rosemary Cox is an experienced aerobics teacher who has details of classes in the area:

ROSEMARY COX
Egham (87) 33610
4 Runnymede Court, Egham

Air Sports & Pleasure Flights

Flying Lessons

FAIROAKS AIRPORT
Map 1 Bc
Chobham (09905) 8075
2½m E Chobham on A319
Flying Lessons: telephone for details
See Pleasure Flights: E.A.A. Aviation

Plain Spotting

BLACKBUSHE AIRPORT
Map 1 Ba
Yateley (0252) 873331
Yateley, 2m W Camberley off A30
Open: all year, daily
Free
Popular site with spotters, all aviation activities can be viewed from car park; used only by light aircraft with a few wartime aeroplanes in hangars, A.G.U. 52 on apron for viewing
P ✕

HEATHROW AIRPORT
Map 1 Ac
(01) 759 7224
3m NE Staines off A4
Spectator roof garden, Queen's
Building, between Terminal 1 &
2
Open: all year, daily 10.00-dusk
(closed 25 & 26 Dec)
Charge: 50p (ch15 20p)
Amusement arcade, children's
play area
🅿 🛄 🚹 ♀

Pleasure Flights

E.A.A. AVIATION
Map 1 Bc
Chobham (09905) 8075
Fairoaks Airport, Chobham
2½m E Chobham on A319
Open: daily by arrangement
Charge: 'See Surrey from Air'.
Fairoaks to Guildford, 20 mins
£9 per seat (longer trips
available); 'See London from
Air', 40 mins (telephone for
details)

Angling

Organisations

**NATIONAL FEDERATION OF
ANGLERS**
Derby (0332) 362000
Halliday House, 2 Wilson St,
Derby DE1 1PG
The governing body for coarse
angling in Britain. Membership
is through clubs and
associations. 420 such
organisations are affiliated
representing some 450,00
coarse anglers.

**SALMON & TROUT
ASSOCIATION**
01-283 5838
Fishmongers Hall, London
Bridge, London EC4R 9EL
National body for game fishing,
has over 70 branches in Britain
and over 200,000 members.

**NATIONAL ANGLERS'
COUNCIL**
Peterborough (0733) 54084
11 Cowgate, Peterborough PE1
1LZ
Governing body for angling (all
types) in England. Runs National
Angling Coaching scheme and a
Proficiency Awards scheme,
designed to improve the
proficiency of anglers, with
special emphasis on ecology
and protection of the water
environment.

CENTRAL ASSOCIATION OF LONDON & PROVINCIAL ANGLING CLUBS
01-686 3199
9 Kemble Rd, Croydon, Surrey
Members and affiliated clubs can use the waters which the association either owns or rents. They also provide an Anglers' Guide to these waters.

See also Angling Clubs

Rod Licences

THAMES WATER AUTHORITY (T.W.A.)
01-837 3300
Head Office, New River Head, Rosebury Ave., London EC1
The rivers and inland waters of Surrey are controlled by the Thames Water Authority. Anglers using these waters must first obtain an official rod licence. In Surrey rod licences are available from secretaries of most angling clubs (**See** Angling Clubs). from many fishing tackle shops or from the local office of the water authority:
Thames Water Authority
Guildford (0483) 77655
Ladymead, By pass Roads, Guildford

Permits

Almost all rivers and stillwaters are privately owned or controlled by an authority. One important reason for joining an angling club is that members will have access to good waters which are not open to the public.

Some waters are accessible only to members of particular clubs but in many cases a permit can be obtained which allows fishing. These permits are for a day, a week or a season and are usually available from the angling clubs who control the waters, from bailiffs on the banks or from local shops.

In the following section, Where to fish, the clubs, or others, who control the waters are listed below each entry. For the addresses and telephone numbers of club secretaries see Angling Clubs.

If permits can be obtained elsewhere this information is also given.

Where to Fish

Some of the following information is taken from **The Fishing Handbook** (1983 edition), a comprehensive, annual guide to all angling organisations and locations in Britain and Ireland. It includes a guide to day permit fishing and to sea fishing, a list of angling clubs and a directory of suppliers. Three smaller publications separate information for Coarse Fishing, Game Fishing and Sea Fishing. For further details contact:
Beacon Publishing
Northampton (0604) 407288
Jubilee House, Billing Brook Rd,
Weston Favell, Northampton

Coarse Fishing: Rivers

RIVER MOLE
The Mole rises near Betchworth and meanders northwest, winding its way through Dorking, Leatherhead, Cobham and Esher before joining the Thames near Hampton Court. It is a narrow waterway which varies in appearance from deep slow trenches to fast shallow runs. Contains a good head of chubb, dace and roach.
Permits: Deepdene Fisheries
Dorking (0306) 882407
Permits also available from bailiff on bank.

RIVER THAMES
The second largest river in England rises in the Cotswolds near Cirencester and enters Surrey north of Runnymede, flowing east through Staines and Kingston-upon-Thames. There are miles of free fishing from towpaths, courtesy of the ancient rights bestowed upon the people by the Magna Carta. All anglers fishing the Thames however require a rod licence. Fishing in weirpools on the river is controlled by the issue of a permit specifically for these places. **Free Fishing:**
Runnymede House to Bell Weir Lock, right bank
Boundary downstream from Staines, all accessible banks
Permits: application for weir permits for Boveney Lock, Bell Weir Lock, Shepperton, Sunbury and Molesley are available from:
The Thames Water Authority
0734-593333
Finance Department, Nugent House, Vastern Rd, Reading, Berkshire
For further information anglers may contact:
The Thames Angling Preservation Society
The Pines, Tile Kiln Lane, Bexley, Kent DA5 2BB

RIVER WEY

The River Wey, one of the longer Thames tributaries, rises near Alton in Hampshire and meanders north-east through the North Downs to Farnham, through Godalming, Guildford and Byfleet before entering the Thames at Weybridge. It boasts some fine trout in the higher reaches but is predominantly coarse fishing. The river is well stocked with grayling, bream and roach.

Permits: day permits from A & G Allchorne, Tackle dealer, 42 Bridge St, Godalming; Hungerford Sports, 21 High St, Hungerford; Woking & District A.A.; in advance from J. Cobbett, Woodlands, Coldharbour Rd, Pyrford; boundary from Shalford to Send, day permits from bailiff on bank

Canals

BASINGSTOKE CANAL

The Basingstoke Canal links Basingstoke with Woking via Aldershot providing mainly coarse fishing. The Canal is still to be renovated but there is some fishing in the Mytchett area

Permits: from bailiff on bank, day permits T.W.A.

WEY NAVIGATION

9 miles of canal from Newark Bridge, Ripley to Thames Lock, Weybridge
chub, roach, bleak, cudgeon and carp

Permits: day permits available

Stillwaters

BOLDERMERE

Ockham Common, nr Wisley
Bream, roach and pike
Permits: to be let by tender to a club, day permits will be available from: Surrey County Council
01-549 6111
Kingston-upon-Thames

BRITTENS POND

Jacobswell near Guildford
Common and crucian carp, tench and roach
Permits: day permits available from bailiff on bank

EARLSWOOD LAKES

Woodhatch, near Reigate
Mixed coarse fish, notably carp
Permits: not required

FOUR WENTS POND

Holmwood, Dorking
Mixed coarse fish including carp and perch
Permits: not required

FRENSHAM GREAT POND

Frensham
Tench, roach, pike and perch
Permits: Farnham A.S.

FRENSHAM SMALL POND

Frensham Country Park
Tench, rudd, roach, pike, perch and carp
Permits: Farnham A.S.

LANGHAM POND

Runnymede
Roach, tench & pike
Permits: day permits, Windsor Angling Centre, 157 St Leonards Rd, Windsor
(075 35) 67210

LODGE POND
2m SW Farnham
Roach, tench, pike and carp
Permits: Farnham A.S., Forestry
Commission Office

MILL POND
Addlestone
Mixed coarse fish
Permits: Mill Office (0932)
52944

MYTCHETT FARM LAKE
1m NE Farnborough
Bream, roach, tench, pike and
crucian carp
Permits: Raison Bros. Tackle
Shop, Farnborough (0252)
543470

OLD BURY HILL LAKE
Westcott, Dorking
Pike, carp, zander, tench
Permits: available on site or by
post from: Lakeview, Old Bury
Hill, Westcott, Dorking

SILVERMERE LAKE
1½m NW Cobham
Bream with occasional carp &
pike
Permits: Silvermere Golf &
Country Club (09326) 7275

TRILAKES
Sandhurst
Mixed coarse fish
Permits: Trilakes Ltd,
Sandhurst (0252) 873191

VIRGINIA WATER LAKE
Windsor Great Park
Permits: Season ticket from:
Crown Estate's Officer

WAGGONERS WELLS LAKE
Grayshott
Coarse lake contains roach,
perch and carp
Permits: The Ranger,
Summerdean, near Grayshott,
Hindhead

WEY FARM
Oltershaw
Roach, tench, perch and carp
Permits: G. Rowles Lakeview,
Old Bury Hill, Westcott; local
tackle dealers, from house at
entrance to fisheries

Game Fishing: Rivers

RIVER TILLINGBOURNE
Located N of Leith Hill flowing
NE to Shalford to join the Wey
Rainbow trout fishing (any
method) between Chilworth and
Albury
Permits: Tillingbourne Trout
Farm, Albury Mill, Albury (048
641) 2567

RIVER WEY
From Godalming Town Bridge
down to Broadford Bridge,
Shalford, left bank
Roach, dace, chub, perch, pike
with carp, bream and trout
Permits: day permits available
from A & G Allchorne, Tackle
Dealer, 42 Bridge St, Godalming

Stillwaters

RUSHMOOR TROUT LAKE
Rainbow and brown trout
Permits: Benwoods, Edgeware
Rd, London (01) 923 9970;
Sporting Guns, Haslemere
(0428) 51913

TILLINGBOURNE FISHERIES
Blacksmith Lane, Chilworth
Lake and port of R.
Tillingbourne stocked with
rainbow trout, brown and brook
trout
Permits: limited number of day
permits telephone (0483)
33407 or (0483) 577360

TRILAKES
Sandhurst
Permits: Trilakes Ltd (0252)
873191

WAGGONERS WELLS LAKES
Grayshott
Trout lake stocked with brown
and rainbow trout
Permits: The Ranger,
Summerdean, near Grayshott,
Hindhead

WILLINGHURST FISHERY
Shamley Green
4 lakes stocked with rainbow
and brown trout
Permits: limited day permits
from Mr M Syms (04866)
71238

WONERSH TROUT FISHERY
Chilworth
Lake and part of R. Tillingbourne
stocked with rainbow, brown
and brook trout
Permits: limited day permits
from (0483) 33407

Coarse Angling Clubs

Abbreviations:
A. Angling
A.A. Angling Association
C. Club
F. Fishing
P. Preservation
S. Society

BASINGSTOKE CANAL A.A.
Secretary: M. Hatcher
Woking (048 62) 69736
80 Hillview Court, Guildford Rd,
Woking
Membership: through affiliated
clubs

BYFLEET A.A.
Secretary: L. Chapman
Byfleet (09323) 45414
43 Edengrove Rd, Byfleet
Members: 650
Membership: restricted
Facilities: stretches of R. Wey

CARSHALTON & DISTRICT A.S.
Secretary: J.F. Humm
01-644 2830
39 St Albans Rd, Cheam
Formed: 1919
Members: 200
Membership: unrestricted
Facilities: stretch of R. Mole at Betchworth

COBHAM COURT A.S.
Secretary: P. Aspin
Cobham (093 26) 2450
Homelea, Oakfield Rd, Cobham

EPSOM A.S.
Secretary: J.C.J. Wood
Epsom (037 27) 24839
Ashlea, 26 Temple Rd, Epsom
KP19 8HA
Formed: 1890
Members: 332
Membership: unrestricted, junior membership available
Facilities: Two stretches of the Rivers Mole and Wey, at Esher and Weybridge; good head of all coarse fish, occasional brown trout

FISHERS FARM A.C. (F.W.S.)
Secretary: P. Martin
Croydon (0689) 41833
8 Stowell Ave., New Addington, Croydon
Formed: 975
Members: 80
Membership: unrestricted
Facilities: own stretch of water at Chiddingstone

GODALMING A.S.
Secretary: M.R. Richardson
Godalming (048 68) 22791
87 Summers Rd, Farncombe, Godalming GO7 3BE
Members: 1000 senior, 700 junior
Membership: restricted
Facilities: R. Wey 8 miles, 2 coarse lakes; carp, tench, crucians, roach; 2 trout lakes at Winkworth Arboretum

GUILDFORD A.S.
Secretary: G. Pank
01-337 5692
Formed: 1883
Members: 600
Membership: unrestricted, junior membership available
Facilities: R. Wey, most of the fishing rights between Broadford Bridge, Shulford to Triggs Lock, Sutton Green approx. 7 miles of bank; Britten's Pond, Worplesdon carp lake; waters available for exclusive use by visiting clubs are from Broadford Bridge to Stoke Wier

HORLEY PISCATORIAL SOCIETY
Secretary: D.J. Penny
Horley (029 34) 71836
63 Upfield, Horley
Facilities: 2 stretches of the R. Mole and stillwaters

LEATHERHEAD & DISTRICT A.S.
Secretary: R. Boychuk
Leatherhead (037 23) 76771
22 Poplar Ave, Leatherhead
Formed: 1946
Members: 653
Membership: unrestricted
Facilities: R. Mole, approx. 3 miles of bank, 3 local ponds, member of Group Angling Alliance offering 3 large pits, R. Thames and 2 streams

LEISURE SPORT A.S.
Manager: J. Newby
Thorpe Water Park, Staines Lane, Chertsey
Facilities: extensive waters throughout the Thames area

REIGATE & DISTRICT A.A.
Secretary: Mr. D.J. Watts
Reigate (073 72)41977
20 Priory Rd, South Park, Reigate
Members: 70
Membership: unrestricted
Facilities: stretches of the R. Mole at Bury's Court, Flanchford, Santon Wonham, also stretches of water at Stamford Brook at Worplesdon

STAINES A.S.
Secretary: G.H. Brown
01-890 0261
Formed: 1970
Members: 65
Membership: unrestricted
Facilities: 3 gravel pits and R. Colne

THAMES FISHERIES CONSULTATIVE COUNCIL
Secretary: A. Leaver
01-648 5424
11 Chalgrove Ave., Morden

WALTON-ON-THAMES A.S.
Secretary: M.L.Campbell
4 Hennel Close, Dacres Rd, London SE23
Formed: 1896
Members: 120
Membership: restricted
Facilities: private lake and stretch of small stream fishing at Woking, private lake and stretch of the R. Mole at Cobham

WEY NAVIGATION A. AMALGAMATION
Secretary: I. Fraser
Weybridge (0932) 49230
4 Elmgrove Rd, Weybridge KT13 8NZ
Formed: 1968
Members: 500
Membership: unrestricted
Facilities: 9 miles of slow running Wey Navigation Canal from Thames Lock Weybridge, to Newark Bridge, Ripley; chub, roach, bleak, gudgeon, carp; available to hire for matches

WEYBRIDGE A.C.
Secretary: P. Dayman
Addlestone (0932) 53542
61 Byron Rd, Addlestone
Formed: 1900
Members: 450
Membership: restricted
Facilities: R. Wey, 1000 yards upstream of Wey Bridge (Wey Meadows), roach, chub, carp; Wey Navigation Canal; 11 miles beginning at Weybridge, Broadwater Lake, Outlands Park (members only)

WOKING & DISTRICT A.A.
Secretary: B.E. Candler
Woking (04867) 81485
Members: 1020
Membership: restricted

Game Angling Clubs

GODALMING A.S.
Secretary: M.R. Richardson
Godalming (048 68) 22791
87 Summers Rd, Farncombe,
Godalming GO7 3BE

PEPER HAROW PARK FLY F.C.
Secretary: Ms M.E. Hide
Godalming (048 68) 7954
Tanglewood, Moushill Lane,
Milford, Godalming
Formed: 1946
Members: 30
Membership: restricted
Facilities: the water from
Somerset bridges on the
Elstead-Shackleford Rd
downstream to the road bridge
on the A3 at Eashing. Both
banks may be fished except a
small stretch on the North Bank,
bordering Peper Harow
Community and there are three
ponds at Oxenford Farm, the
smallest pond being reserved
for dry fly fishing only
Ends Surrey 1 Approx 760
lines

Antiques

There are a wealth of antique
shops, galleries, markets and
auction rooms in Surrey.
Whatever your taste in antiques
you should enjoy 'hunting'
around for bargains.

In most towns and villages
there are a wealth of antique
and secondhand shops. It would
be impossible to list them all so
a selection are included here.

The British Antique Dealers
Association's main aim is to
establish and maintain
confidence between its
members and the public both in
buying and selling. Unlike a
market stall a member of the
Association will guarantee the
authenticity of an article sold
and will refund money if the
description proves false. The
dealers listed below are
members of The British Antique
Dealer's Association in Surrey.

THE BRITISH ANTIQUE DEALER'S ASSOCIATION
(01) 589 4128
20 Rutland Gate, London SW7

Antique Dealers

BYFLEET
Ronald A. Lee
Byfleet (91) 43346
The Manor House, Byfleet
Open: by arrangement only
Antiques, works of art, clocks,
barometers, furniture

CRANLEIGH
Mann David & Sons Ltd
Cranleigh (048 66) 3777
High Street
Furniture, carpets, rugs,
porcelain, pottery, ceramics

GODALMING
Heath-Bullock
Godalming (048 68)
22562
8 Meadrow,
Godalming
Bygones, curiosities, unusual
items, furniture

GUILDFORD
G. Oliver & Sons
Guildford (0483) 75427
St Catherines House,
Portsmouth Rd
Antiques, works of art,
architectural items, furniture,
glass, porcelain, silver, old
Sheffield plate

KINGSTON-UPON-THAMES
Kingston Antiques
(01) 546 221
138 London Rd
Clocks, barometers, scientific
instruments

WEYBRIDGE
R. Saunders
Weybridge (97) 42601
71 Queen's Rd
Furniture, glass, drawings,
prints, engravings, porcelain,
ceramics, silver

Auctioneers

BLETCHINGLEY
Lawrence's Fine Art Auctioneers
Godstone (0883) 843323
Norfolk House, 80 High St
Open: sales every 6 weeks,
Tue, Wed & Thur
Preview: Fri & Sat before sale
Contents: antiques, bric-a-brac,
some household goods

CHOBHAM
Barber's Fine Art Auctions Ltd
Chobham (09905) 7341
Town Mill, Bagshot Rd
Open: sales every 5 weeks,
Mon
Preview: Fri & Sat before sale
Contents: fine art

DORKING
P. F. Windibank
Dorking (0306) 884556
18-20 Reigate Rd, Dorking
Auction rooms at the Dorking
Halls
Open: sales selected Sat in
month
Preview: day before sale
Contents: mainly antiques

White & Sons
Dorking (0306) 887654
104 High St, Dorking
Auction rooms at Dorking
Market off the High St
Open: sales alternate Mons
Preview: day of sale
Contents: antiques, bric-a-brac
& domestic

GODALMING
Messenger May Baverstock
Godalming (048 68) 23567
93 High St, Godalming
Open: monthly, Weds & Thur
Contents: fine art & antiques

GUILDFORD
Clark-Gammon
Guildford (0483) 72266
High St, Guildford
Auction rooms at Bedford Rd
Open: selected Tue in month
Contents: fine art & household
goods

MERSTHAM
Harold Williams Bennett &
Partners
Merstham (073 74) 2234/5
Auction rooms at village hall,
Station Approach
Open: selected Thur in month
Preview: Wed before sale
Contents: junk, household,
antiques & brica-brac

VIRGINIA WATER
Wentworth Auction
Galleries
Wentworth (099 04) 3711
21 Station Approach
Open: Weds, every 5 weeks
Preview: day before sale
Contents: antique & quality
furniture

Antique Fairs

See Events: October

Aquarium

UNDERWATER WORLD
See Zoos: Birdworld

Art Galleries

BOURNE HALL MUSEUM
See Museums: Bourne Hall
Museum

GOMSHALL MILL & GALLERY
See Mills: Gomshall Mill &
Gallery

GUILDFORD HOUSE GALLERY
Map 2 Ab /p60
Guildford (0483) 32133
155 High St, Guildford
Open: all year, Mon-Sat 10.30-
17.00 (telephone in advance)
Free
No dogs
See also Historic Homes:
Guildford House Gallery

THE PICTURE GALLERY
Map 1 Ac /p39
Egham (87) 34455
Royal Holloway College, Egham
Hill on A30
Open: all year by arrangement
in writing
Charge: 50p
No dogs
🅿 ♿

SUTTON PLACE
Map 2 Ac
Guildford (0483) 504455
Guildford, 2m N Guildford off
A3
Open: All year. Wed–Sun by
arrangement
Charge: £4 (students £2)
includes house, exhibition &
garden; £1.50 (£1) exhibition
only
No dogs
**See also Historic Homes &
Gardens:** Sutton Place

THE WATTS GALLERY
Map 2 Ab /p26
Guildford (0483) 810235
Compton, 3m NW Guildford off
B3000
Open: all year, daily (closed
Thurs); Nov-Feb 14.00-18.00;
March-Oct 14.00-16.00; all
year, Wed & Sat 11.00-13.00
Free (donations gratefully
accepted)
🅿 ♿

Bird Reserves

ROYAL SOCIETY FOR THE
PROTECTION OF BIRDS
The Lodge, Sandy, Beds SG19
2DL
The RSPB is a charity and part
of its work involves managing
85 bird reserves in Great Britain.
The aim of these reserves is the
conservation of birds and their
habitat. The RSPB organises
many activities connected with
birdwatching and bird
conservation. There is a special
organisation for young people:
Young Ornithologist Club (YOC).

If you would like to know
more about the RSPB and YOC,
if you would like to make a
donation or to become a
member contact the address
above.

The following list of reserves
in Surrey are free to members
of the RSPB but there is
sometimes a charge for the
general public. When visiting
reserves remember that they are
there for the birds so do nothing
which would in any way disturb
them or harm their environment.
Always keep to marked paths.
Reserves are closed on Nov 2-5
and Dec 25-26.

Bird Watching

BARFOLD COPSE
Map 2 Bb
2m SE Haslemere off B2131
Access via footpath from 2nd
Black Down turning on B2131
Open: all year
13 acres of mixed deciduous
woodland, typical bird species
include black cap, willow
warbler & spotted
flycatcher
Marked nature trail

RSPBA

BAY POND
See Nature Reserves: Bay
Pond

BIRDWORLD
Map 2 Bb

Bentley (0420) 22140
Holt Pound, 3m SW Farnham
on A325
Open: all year, daily 9.30-18.00
or dusk (closed 25 Dec)
Charge: bird garden £1.30 (ch
85p), aquarium 45p (ch 35p)

Zoological bird gardens &
aquarium
No dogs
P ⚑ ♿ ▭

BIRDWORLD
See Zoos: Birdworld

BUSBRIDGE LAKE
See Nature Reserves:
Busbridge Lake

THE CHART
Map 4 Ac
Limpsfield, 2m SE town on
B269
Beautiful expanse of heath and
mixed woodland with varied
plants and unusual birds
including nightjars, woodlarks
and woodcocks
FC P ⚏

CHOBHAM COMMON
Map 1 Bb
3m SW Egham off A30
1,600 acres of heath and
woodland with variety of birds
including meadow pipit, skylark
& carrion crow
SCC ℗ ⌒

GATWICK ZOO AND AVIARIES
Map 4 Ab
See Zoos: Gatwick Zoo and
Aviaries

FRENSHAM PONDS
Map 2 Aa
Frensham Common, 3m S
Farnham on A287
Originally a source of fish for
Farnham Castle, now part of
Frensham Country Park with
lush vegetation and moats
affording excellent nesting sites
for birds
Waverley District Council
See also Country Parks:
Frensham Country Park

RANMORE COMMON
See Country Parks: Ranmore
Common

STAINES RESERVOIR
Map 1 Ac
N Staines on A30
Open: all year, daily (no permit
required)
Bird watching is allowed only
from the central causeway
between north and south
reservoirs
Designated as site of special
scientific interest with variety of
species including great crested
grebe, cossander, coot and teal

VIRGINIA WATER
Map 1 Ab
1½m SW Egham on A30
Attractive lake in woodland,
species include mandarin duck,
garganey, pochard, siskin and
hawfinch
See also Bird Reserves, Nature
Reserves, Woodland, Zoos

Boating

RIVER WEY & GODALMING NAVIGATIONS

The River Wey rises from two sources in Hampshire and the Surrey uplands, flows NE past Godalming and Guildford, finally joining the Thames at Weybridge. Like many navigable rivers it was originally designed as a trade route in 1651. After a period of commercial boom in the late 18th and early 19th centuries, its importance gradually declined in the face of fierce competition from the new railway companies. By 1949 the Wey Navigation's role as a commercial carrier was almost at an end. However, it remained part of the water management scheme for flood control in the valley and in 1964 it was donated to the National Trust, as was the Godalming Navigation in 1968. Although some of the characteristics remain of a navigable river once conducting trade, today it affords opportunities for leisure and recreation including canoeing, sailing, fishing and river trips. Details of these can be found in other sections of the Leisure A-Z. **See** Canoeing, Sailing, Fishing, River Trips

All craft using the navigations require a licence and insurance. Licences are available from:
The National Trust River Wey & Godalming Navigations
Dapdune Lea, Wharf Road, Guildford

RIVER THAMES

The River Thames stretches for 124 miles from Lechdale to Teddington. The non-tidal section of the river forms a unique waterway which offers a wide range of leisure and recreational activities. There is beautiful scenery, fishing, sailing and river trips.

The control and management of the river system is carried out by Thames Water. All pleasure boats must be registered before being used in any way.

Application forms for boat registration are available from:
The Finance Director
Income Section
Thames Water
Nugent House
Vastern Road, Reading

Thames Water also publish leaflets on all recreational facilities available on the Thames. For general information on recreational facilities please contact:
Amenity and Recreation Officer
Thames Water
Nugent House
Vastern Road, Reading

An excellent free guide entitled **The Thames Royal River** is available from:
The Thames and Chilterns Tourist Board,
Hoseseasons
See also Angling, Sailing, River Trips

Boat Hire

BYFLEET BOATHOUSE
Byfleet (91) 40828
On the old Parvis Bridge Rd,
Byfleet
Open: Easter-end Sep
Rowing Boats: £10 deposit,
£2 hour
Membership also available with
facilities including workshop,
storage, club activities

GODALMING NARROW BOATS
Godalming (048 68) 21306
Farncombe Boathouse,
Cattershall Lock
Open: all year, daily 9.00-18.00
Rowing Boats: £15 deposit all
craft, £3 hour, £10 day

Punts: £30 deposit, £5 hour,
£20 day
Narrow Boats: £40 day
Launches: 6 seats from £6
hour, £25 day

GUILDFORD BOATHOUSE
Guildford (0483) 504494
Millbrook, Guildford
Open: Easter-end Sep, daily
9.00-18.00
Canoes: £10 deposit all craft,
£1 hour Mon-Sat; £1.25 hour
w/ends & BHs
Rowing Boats: £2.50 hour
Mon-Sat; £3 hour w/ends &
BHs
See also: River Trips

Canoeing

Although it is possible to enjoy canoeing without belonging to a club, many inland waterways, backwaters and mill streams are private property and not open to the general public but some are open to clubs. It is also safer to undertake any water sport as part of an organised group. For further information contact The British Canoe Union which is the governing body for the sport in this country. The 20 mile stretch of water known as the Wey and Godalming navigation is canoeable in both directions from Weybridge to Godalming.

THE BRITISH CANOE UNION
Weybridge (0932) 41341

Canoe Hire

BYFLEET BOATHOUSE
Byfleet (91) 40828
The Old Parvis Bridge Rd,
Byfleet

Courses

**SHEPPERTON CANOE
SCHOOL**
Walton-on-Thames (98)
247978
c/o Whitewater Sports,
Shepperton Marina, Felix Lane,
Shepperton
Courses: beginners one day
course, w/ends 10.00-16.30
Charge: £15 (beginners course
including canoe & buoyancy
aids)

Caravan & Camping Sites

CARAVANS
Any reference in this section to caravans is to touring caravans, not to permanent vans. Some of the sites will have permanent caravans for hire (perhaps being very large holiday camp caravan parks) while others are open only to touring caravans, dormobiles & tents. If you have a preference for a particular type of caravan park always telephone ahead to check.

TENTS
Tents are admitted to the following camping and caravan sites where indicated.

CHARGES
Charges given are for one day/night. Unless otherwise indicted charges for caravans & tents include a car; charges for caravans, tents & dormobiles include two people. There may be a range of charges for tents depending on size.

LOCATIONS
The sites are listed under the nearest town.

Laleham

LALEHAM PARK CAMPING SITE
Map 1 Ac
Chertsey (093 28) 64149
Abbey Drive, Laleham
Open: early April-early Oct
Pitches: 9 caravans; 80 tents
Charges: caravans 90p per person (ch16 45p); tents 70p per person (ch16 35p)
Playground, dogs on leads

Albury

EDGELEY CARAVAN PARK
Map 2 Ac
Shere (048 641) 2129
Farley Green, Albury, 4½m SE Guildford 1m N of A248
Pitches: 40 (total) caravans, tents & dormobiles
Charge: £2.50 per pitch
No dogs

Godalming

MERRY HARRIERS
Map 2 Bb
Wormley (042 879) 2883
Hambledon, 4m S Godalming off A283
Pitches: 20-30 (total) caravans & tents
Charge: £1.50 per pitch, 50p each extra adult (ch 25p)
Quiet site, dogs on leads

Castles

BLETCHINGLEY CASTLE
Map 4 Ab/p17
½m E Reigate
Not open to public
Masonry destroyed by Henry III's stone bombards during 13th century, only earthworks remain

FARNHAM CASTLE
Map 2 Aa/p47
Castle Hill, Farnham
Open: April-Sep standard DofE, see p5
Charge: 30p (ch & OAPs 15p)
DofE

GUILDFORD CASTLE
Map 2 Ab /p61
Guildford (0483) 505050
Castle St, Guildford
Open: April-Sep, daily 11.00-18.00
Charge: 30p (ch 15p)
Dogs on lead
See also Gardens: Guildford Castle
🏠 ♿

Church Buildings

BISHOP'S PALACE
Map 2 Aa /p47
Farnham (0252) 721194
Farnham Castle, Farnham
Open: all year, Wed 14.00-16.00 (closed Christmas week); groups (12) at other times by arrangement
Charge: 40p (ch 20p), group reductions, all visitors guided
No dogs
🅿 🏠

CHERTSEY ABBEY (RUINS)
Map 1 Ac
Chertsey, N outskirts of town
Founded in AD 666 but destroyed successively by the Danes and Henry VIII in the Dissolution of the Monasteries; recent excavations in the ruins have revealed kilns in which the beautiful Chertsey tiles were made

GUILDFORD CATHEDRAL
Map 2 Ab /p58
Guildford (0483) 64722
Stag Hill, Guildford
Open: all year, daily; summer 9.30-17.00 (winter 16.00)
Free
🅿 🏠 ♿ 🍽

WAVERLEY ABBEY
Map 2 Ab /p49
2m SE Farnham off B3001
Not open to public
Ruins of the first Cistercian Abbey in England, founded in the 12th century; currently under restoration and to be re-opened though date uncertain
DofE

Country Parks

Unless otherwise stated parks are open all year, daily and are free. There is sometimes a small charge for car parks

BOX HILL
Map 4 Aa/p83
1m N Dorking off A24
800 acres of woods and chalk downland rising to 400ft from the R. Mole on the edge of the North Downs; commands magnificent views, nature trails
Open: April-Oct, Wed-Sun & BHs 13.30-17.30; Nov-mid Dec, Wed, Thur & w/ends 14.00-16.00
Dogs on leads
🅿 ⛺ ♿ ⛽ ✕

CHOBHAM COMMON
Map 1 Bb
2m NW Chobham off B386/A30
1,600 acres heathland and woodland with fine views
See also Bird Watching: Chobham Common
🅿 ♿

COLLEY HILL
Map 4 Ab
½m N Reigate W of A217
Open downland on steep chalk escarpment, capped with woodland, fine views
Lavatories
🅿 ☕

DEVIL'S PUNCHBOWL
See Hindhead
NT

EPSOM COMMON
Map 3 Ba/p41
Dorking Rd, Epsom 1½m W Epsom off B280
400 acres grassland & woodland with excellent views across Surrey hills to Mole Gap
Fishing, horseriding, nature trails (leaflet available from Parks Dpt), Nature Reserve, nature w/end during summer (telephone Park Dpt for details)
🅿 ⛺

EPSOM & WALTON DOWNS
Map 3 Bb
1m S Epsom off B290
600 acres S Epsom with good views, footpaths, nature trail (leaflet available from Town Hall & Park Dpt); racecourse and Derby meeting
🅿 ☕

FRENSHAM COUNTRY PARK
Map 2 Ba/p50
3m S Farnham on A287
Open heathland interspersed with pine & birch woodland; self guided conservation trail at Great Pond car park
Open: all year, daily
See also Bird Watching: Frensham Ponds
🅿 ☕

HINDHEAD
Map 2 Bb /p67
2m NE Haslemere off A3
1,000 acres of heath and
woodland focused on 895ft
Gibbet Hill and Devil's
Punchbowl, a heath filled arena
to NE of the common;
magnificent views, nature trail
(leaflet available from car park)
Lavatories
NT ▣ ⌣

HOG'S BACK
Map 2 Ab
3½m W Guildford on A31
Name given to road between
Guildford & Farnham, tracing
the ridge above the surrounding
countryside
▣ ⊨

HOGSMILL
Map 3 Bb /p45
1m N Ewell
Grassy, tree lined meadow
following course of Hogsmill
River from its source in Ewell
village; good walking

HORTON COUNTRY PARK
Map 3 Ba /p41
1m NW Epsom, 1½m S of
Ewell off B284
400 acres of agricultural
countryside & woodland;
information centre, nature trails
Guided walk April-Sep, second
Sun in month, leaving 14.30
from main car park
▣ ⅋ ⊨

HYDONS HEATH & HYDONS BALL
Map 2 Bb
3m S Godalming, 1½m W of
B2130
125 acres of heath and
woodland, excellent views from
summit
NT ▣

LALEHAM PARK
Map 1 Ac
Laleham, ½m N Chertsey on
B376
76 acres of recreational grounds
with wooded walks and picnic
areas
Spellthorne District Council
Lavatories
SCC ▣ ⅋ ⌣ ⊨

LEITH HILL
Map 4 Aa /p86
4m S Dorking off B2126
Pine woods with footpaths; the
tower on Leith Hill is the
highest point in SE England
with magnificent views of the
Channel and countryside
Tower open March-Oct on fine
days
NT SCC ⌣

LIGHTWATER COUNTRY PARK
Map 1 Bb
2½m NE Camberley off junction
of M3 & A322
120 acres recreation area; self
guided nature trail (leaflet
available Surrey Heath Borough
Council); good views
Lavatories
▣ ⊨

RANMORE COMMON
Map 4 Aa / p31
½m NW Dorking
470 acres open chalk grass and woodlands, good for bird watching; 2½m forest trail
See also Orienteering: Ranmore Common
NT FC ⊑ ⊼

RUNNYMEDE COUNTRY PARK
Map 1 Ac / p96
1 m NW Egham on A308
200 acres of meadow on banks of the Thames where King John signed the Magna Carta in 1215; Magna Carta Memorial, Kennedy Memorial & Commonwealth Air Forces Memorial on Cooper's Hill; gatehouse designed by Edward Luytens housing tearoom; river trips
See also Boating: Runnymede Boathouse
Lavatories
Dogs on leads
NT 🅿 ⅃ ⊑ ⊼

WINDSOR GREAT PARK
Map 1 Ab / p101
Off A328/A30
Accessible via Wick Lane, Englefield Green, near Egham
See Savill Gardens and Valley Gardens

WITLEY COMMON
Map 2 Bb
7m SW Guildford
Information Centre set in pine woods on edge of Common; audio visual displays and exhibitions; nature trails start here leading to open heath and woodland; guided walks by arrangement with warden, groups must be accompanied by centre guide
Open: March & Nov, w/ends 11.00-16.00; April-Oct, Tue-Sun & BHs 11.00-13.00 & 14.00-17.00
See also Woodland: Witley Common
NT 🅿 ⅃ ⅃

Crafts

Organisation

SOUTH EAST ARTS
Tunbridge Wells (0892) 41666
9-10 Crescent Rd, Tunbridge Wells, TN1 2LU
The Regional Arts Association for Surrey, Kent & East Sussex

Potteries

CRANLEIGH POTTERY
Donald Marsh, The Old School, High St, Cranleigh
Open: all year, w/days
Oxidised stoneware thrown to order

GOMSHALL MILL POTTERY
Shere (048 641) 2433
Gomshall, nr Guildford
Open: all year, daily (except
Mon) 10.00-17.30
Commercial pottery shop selling
wide range of production
potter's work; domestic pottery,
earthenware, stoneware &
commemorative pieces,
miniature dolls & macrame.
See also Mills: Gomshall Mill
and Gallery

SHERE POTTER
Shere (048 641) 2625
Lower St, Shere
Open: all year, w/days 9.00-
17.30; Sat 9.15-17.30 & Sun
10.00-18.00
Domestic stoneware pottery
produces by Chris Otway on
premises, also small collection
of jewellery, macrame and
basketry

ROSE POTTERY
Woking (048 62) 63223
Ruxley House, 28 Mount
Hermon Rd, Woking
Open: anytime
Variety of pottery handmade on
premises

THE POTTERY STUDIO
Leatherhead (53) 75127
37 Church St, Leatherhead
Handmade pottery, domestic
and individual pieces made on
premises by Eileen Stevens and
work of local potters

WHARF POTTERY
Godalming (048 68) 4097
55 St Johns St, Farncombe
Open: all year, w/days 9.00-
17.00 & Sat 9.00-13.00
Pottery of Mary Wondrauch,
individually hand thrown and
decorated in traditional slip-
trailed earthenware mugs, jugs,
wine jars, also commemorative
plates and plaques

Ironwork

RICHARD QUINNELL LTD
Leatherhead (53) 75148
Rowhurst Forge, Oxshott Rd,
Leatherhead
Open: all year, w/days 9.00-
17.00, Sat 9.00-13.00
Shop attached to forge selling
small items of wrought iron,
specialising in architectural
metal work and restoration of
ancient ironwork

Jewellery

**JIM FOX GOLD & SILVER
DESIGNS**
Guildford (0483) 33484
12 Martyr Rd,
Guildford
Open: all year, Tue-
Sun 9.00-17.00
Jewellery work of Jim Fox &
partner also small amount of
other work on sale

General

HERITAGE CRAFTS
Haslemere (0428) 51902
76 Wey Hill, Haslemere
Open: all year, Thur-Tue 9.00-
17.00, Wed 9.00-13.00
(closed Sun)
Craft shop is a section of a shop
selling art and craft materials,
mainly pottery

NEW ASHGATE GALLERY
Farnham (0252) 3208
Wagon Yard, Farnham
Open: all year, daily 10.00-
17.00 (closed Wed & Sun)
Several rooms exhibiting work
of contemporary artists and
craftsmen; embroidery,
ceramics, glass, jewellery &
knitting

RIDGEWAY HOUSE FARM
Farnham (0252) 23006
Runwick, Farnham
Open: all year, Sat 11.30-
18.00, Sun 11.00-16.00
Traditional country crafts; hand-
blocked textiles, basketry,
patchwork, Dorset buttons, hand
knitted and crochet garments
made from fleece of less well-
known sheep, natural coloured
wool & tweed

ROMANY
20 High St, Haslemere
Open: all year, Mon-Sat 9.30-
17.00, Wed 9.30-13.30
Craftshop specialising in
handmade printed cotton
clothes, handknitted jumpers,
domestic stoneware, stuffed
toys & other small crafts

THE CRAFT SHOP
Tadworth (073 781) 3587
122 South St, Dorking
Open: all year, Tue-Sat 9.30-
17.00 & Wed 9.30-13.00
Small craft shop selling
handmade dolls, toys, turned
wood, wrought iron, leather,
enamel, glass & pottery;
specialises in jewellery

THE HARRIST CRAFTSHOP
Reigate (073 72) 40203
21 West St, Reigate
Open: all year, Mon-Sat 9.00-
17.30, Wed 9.00-13.00
Wide selection of domestic
tableware, also wrought iron,
pewter work, weaving, Batik,
jewellery, woodwork & gallery
with original pictures

TOBYCRAFT GALLERIES
Ripley (048 643) 3349
High St, Ripley
Open: all year, Mon-Sat 9.00-
17.30
Unusual selection of original
paintings, lamps, jewellery,
pottery, wrought iron, leather
goods, welsh tapestry, ponchos,
jackets & bedspreads

Musical Instruments

DOLMETSCH WORKSHOPS
Haslemere (0428) 54320
107 Blackdown, Rural
Industries, Haste, Haste Hill,
Haslemere
Open: all year, telephone in
advance, viewing usually
between 9.00-16.30
The Dolmetsch family
manufacture musical
instruments in this workshop
and factory, including recorders,
lutes, spinets, virginals, viols,
harpsicords and forte-pianos

Cricket

Surrey has been inextricably
linked with cricket since
Elizabethan times. Although
Hambledon in Hampshire
played an important part in
drawing up the rules for the
game in 1777, Surrey has
documentary evidence claiming
that cricket was played there as
far back as 1598. A witness in
a Guildford court testified that
cricket was played by the boys
of the Grammar School in
1550.

Cricket

Surrey has many attractive cricket grounds, including Tilford Green where cricket has been staged for many years. At Headley country ground a game of cricket can be watched without a single building in sight, except the cricket pavilion. The pitch at Holmbury St Mary is one of the most delightfully situated in the county whose pitch and outfield are cut from heathland.

Spectators are always welcome at amateur games, usually every Saturday during the season, which runs from mid April to early September. In first class cricket Surrey County Cricket Club holds the record for winning the County Championship 7 years running. Their home ground is the Oval at Kennington in London which traditionally stages at least one Test Match a year and some of the John Player League, Nat-West and Benson & Hedges championship games

The Centenary Library, located at the Oval, is open to members on match days and at other times by arrangement. For details of membership contact:
The Membership Secretary:
Miss Payne
Surrey County Cricket Club
The Oval, Kennington, London SE11
01-582 6660

Club Cricket

THE CLUB CRICKET CONFERENCE
This organisation produces a handbook containing an official register of 2,000 affiliated clubs and details of their secretaries in the various counties:
Secretary: D.J. Annettes
01-949 4001
353 West Barnes Lane, New Malden

THE SURREY CRICKET ASSOCIATION
01-582 5486
Secretary: B. Hurdle
1 Chestnut Lane, Weybridge
The aim of the Surrey Cricket Association is to encourage club and youth cricket as much as possible. It provides many benefits which will assist all clubs in the County both large and small. The County is divided into regions which run local competitions, seminars and relay the views and needs of individual clubs back to the S.C.A. The Association will also help individuals locate a club in their area:

CROYDON
D. Stevens
01-778 9815
7 Madeline Road, Amberley, London SE10

KINGSTON
A.D.H. Hodgson
18 Southwood Gardens, Hinchley Wood, Esher

LONDON
R Baker
01-733 8109 Brixton Hill Court,
Brixton Hill, London SW2

MERTON
G. Lewis
01-980 0166
131 South Park Road, London
SW19

NORTHWEST REGION
D.W. Guppy
Bagshot (695) 1100
11 Lambourne Drive, Jenkins,
Bagshot

SOUTHEAST REGION
A. Bates
Oxted (088 388) 2310
64 Chestnut Copes, Oxted

SUTTON
E. Clark
01-733 1431
155 Benhill Road, Sutton

Women's Cricket

Women have played cricket for over 200 years, the earliest recorded match being on Gosden Common, Surrey in 1745. Despite Victorian disapproval and lack of organization, the Women's Cricket Association was eventually formed in 1926 and the first representative public match was played in 1929. All women's cricket is amateur status and played under the normal rules governing cricket

THE WOMEN'S CRICKET ASSOCIATION
01-387 3423
16 Upper Woburn Place,
London WC1
The Women's Cricket Association will supply further details, a list of affiliated clubs and an annual fixture list of all representative matches

Youth Cricket

All major clubs in Surrey run colt teams. The junior cricket administrator for Surrey will be able to advise on all aspects of youth cricket:
Mr W.D. Wickson
The Oval, Kennington, London SE11

The S.C.A. and the Surrey Schools Cricket Association have developed, with the sponsorship of the Nestle Co., a joint colts coaching scheme. The 10 week courses take place in October, November and December, ensuring that boys in the 15-16 age groups receive expert coaching under the guidance of qualified staff. For further details of these courses or any other coaching activities within the County contact:
Mr Conrad Clark
01-654 3341
47 Towers View, Shirley, Croydon

Cricket

Indoor Cricket

At present 52 clubs participate in the S.C.A. indoor cricket competition which is staged at Elmbridge, Farnborough, Guildford and Woking leisure centres. Any clubs interested in playing in the competition should contact:
Surrey Cricket Association
01-582 5486
The Oval, Kennington, London SE11

Festival Week

Festival week is held at the Oval, usually towards the end of the cricket season. It includes teams from the county regions together with the winners of the Surrey Cup and the Flora-Dors Cup, as well as an old Surrey XI. The week culminates in the Champion of Champions Shield Final. For further details contact: The S.C.A. Office
01-582 5486

Cricket Coaching

THE SURREY CRICKET SCHOOL AND CRICKET CLUB
01-398 8177
Orchard Lane, East Molesey
Open: all year, daily 9.00-21.00
Facilities: six full size nets; chief coach Geoff Arnold, other qualified coaches always in attendance for private coaching to clubs, schools, individuals or groups; indoor cricket competitions, video and bowling machine; groups coaching sessions every Friday evening and 2-day courses during the school holidays; full size gym, saunas, snooker room
For further details write to the Director, Tony Hodgson
🅿 ♿ ♀

Cycling

Perhaps the most pleasant way of enjoying the countryside is by bicycle. Moving fast enough to present a constantly changing scene whilst allowing time to appreciate the surroundings, this form of transport also combines the advantages of being beneficial to the health with the gratifying sense of getting around under one's own steam. Although many people cycle alone, the social activities and sense of security provided by joining a cycle touring club heighten the enjoyment of this popular sport.

THE CYCLISTS' TOURING CLUB
Godalming (04868) 7217
69 Meadrow, Godalming,
Surrey
A national association representing the interests of all cyclists. Current membership totalling 35,000. All members can receive help on route planning, maps and practical advice on the best areas for cycle touring.
Membership: £10.00 per annum
Includes subscription to bi-monthly magazine and 3rd party insurance. The CTC also produces a handbook including addresses for accomodation, repairs and local representatives.

WEST SURREY DISTRICT ASSOCIATION
Secretary: A. McKenzie
Guildford (0483) 233828
2 Cumberland Avenue, Guildford

EAST SURREY DISTRICT ASSOCIATION
Secretary: H. J. Brazier
Croydon (01) 656 2852
68 Alexander Road,
Addiscombe, Croydon

MOLE VALLEY ASSOCIATION
Secretary: W. G. Budd
Leatherhead (53) 75959
43 Lodge Close, Etcham

Disabled

This section highlights those places and organisations in Surrey which offer special facilities for disabled people. There are many other places which are accessible to disabled visitors and these will be found in the various sections and are marked with the symbol: ♿

Angling

ANGLING FOR THE DISABLED
Contact: Mr M. Richardson
Godalming (048 68) 23635
87 Summers Rd, Farncombe

Disabled

Archery

ARCHERY FOR THE DISABLED
Contact: Mr P. Hilderley
Brookwood (048 67) 3873
77 Sutton Ave, St John's,
Woking

Athletics

ATHLETICS FOR THE DISABLED
Contact: Mr J. Taylor
Aldershot (0252) 23747
13 Yeoman's Close, Manor Rd,
Tongham, Farnham

Bowls

BOWLS FOR THE DISABLED
Contact: Mr S. Vince
Guildford (0483) 69747
191 Epsom Rd, Merrow,
Guildford

THE SWANS
Alexander Recreation Ground,
Epsom
Contact: Mr Cooke
01-397 8390
Any handicapped or blind
people welcome at special
sessions alternate Mondays

Garden

WISLEY GARDENS
See Gardens Wisley Gardens

Sailing

FRENSHAM POND
Contact: Mr D. Dick
Bentley (0420) 23188
preferably during term-time
2 challenge trimarans available
for use by the disabled; Mr Dick
will advise

HORLEY LAKE
See Frensham Pond for details

Sports

BRITISH SPORTS ASSOCIATION FOR THE DISABLED
Hon Development Officer (SE
region):
Mr P. Jamieson
'Fairholme', Mark Beach,
Edenbridge TN8 5NR
Specialist advice and
encouragement organisation
which coordinates activities,
facilities and clubs for disabled
people who want to take part in
sports.

FARNHAM & DISTRICT SPORTS ASSOCIATION FOR THE DISABLED
Secretary: Mrs Jane Hooper
Frensham (025 125) 3135
Activities: swimming, dry
sports (archery, billiards, darts,
carpet bowls, table tennis)
See also Farnham Leisure Centre;
sailing (Frensham Pond),
canoeing (Basingstoke & Fleet
Canal) contact secretary

GUILDFORD ADVENTURERS ASSOCIATION
Secretary: Mr Colin Hassell
Guildford (0483) 505664
Activities: swimming, weight training, running, athletics, gymnastics, trampolining, table tennis, snooker, basket ball
See also: Guildford Sports Centre
For details of the Friday Swimmers' Club contact the Medical Secretary: Guildford (0483) 68997
The Guildford Adventurers welcome both physically and mentally handicapped members

GUILDFORD SPORTS AND SOCIAL CLUB
Secretary: Mrs J. Thomas
Guildford (0483) 60331
Activities usually take place at Lockwood Centre, Guildford
Activities: badminton, basketball, table tennis, billiards, darts and board games; anyone aged 10-40 welcome

GUILDFORD THURSDAY HANDICAPPED CLUB
Secretary: Mrs M. Jarosz
Guildford (0483) 39049
Activities take place at: St Peter's Church Hall, Bellfields, Guildford
Activities: varied entertainments and setting down games; anyone aged 18-70 welcome

THE LEATHERHEAD SWANS
Secretary: Mrs Hardman
Leatherhead (0372) 372131
Activities: swimming, canoeing, table tennis, bowls, dancing, crafts
See also: Leatherhead Leisure Centre
Bowls **See also** Epsom & Dorking Leisure Centres

LITTLETON P.H.A.B.S.A.I.L.
Contact: Mr H. Statham
Woking (048 62) 63289
Sailing trimarans contact:: Mrs Aubin, Woking (048 62) 68143

SURREY P.H.A.B.
Contact: Mr A. Aubin
Felbury House, Holmbury St. Mary, Dorking

WOKING DOLPHINS
Secretary: Mrs. E. Docker
Wentworth (099 04) 3368
Activities: swimming at Woking Centre Pool, all ages welcome

WOKING WIZARDS
Secretary: Mr Geoff Choat
Brookwood (048 67) 81447
Activities: badminton, table tennis, snooker, darts, indoor bowls, wheelchair basket ball, board games
All ages welcome

WOKING P.H.A.B
Secretary: Mrs M. Statham
Woking (048 62) 63289
Weekly social club, anyone aged 8-40 welcome

Woodland and Countryside

CHOBHAM COMMON
Extensive area of heath and woodland with good views from car parks at Staple Hill (S of M3); also picnic tables close to one of the car parks

CHERTSEY MEADS
SE Chertsey, parking by the river's edge where river activities can be watched

NEWLANDS CORNER
The car park here provides one of the best viewpoints in the County across the south and southeast of Surrey.
Lavatories

PUTTENHAM COMMON
3m E Farnham, 1½m S Puttenham
Attractive area of sandy heath and woodland, fine views westwards to Hindhead from car park on eastern edge of site

SHEEPLEAS
SE Horsley
Attractive area of chalk down and woodlands from the car park off Shere Rd

TILBURSTOW HILL
S Godstone
Fine view over largely agricultural land across SE of the country

WOTTON & ABINGER COMMONS
SW Dorking
Extensive area of pine and birch woodland extending from Friday Street in the north to Leith Hill in the south; three attractively sited car parks at Broadmoor, Friday Street and Starveall Corner, though access beyond car parks is difficult for wheelchairs

Riding

DIAMOND HANDICAPPED CENTRE
01-643 7764
Woodmansterne Rd, Carshalton
Open: Tue-Sat
Those wishing to take part must have a certificate signed by G.P. and complete an application form available from the Centre
Lessons: £7.40 per quarter for one lesson per week; £11 for longer rides
23 mounts
See also Riding: Southborough Lodge Farm

Water Skiing

DISABLED WATER SKI ASSOCIATION
Secretary: Mrs Maeve Edge
Ashtead (27) 73046
Warren Wood, Ashtead

Events

Annual events are listed under the month in which they normally occur but for exact dates and further details of events contact local Tourist Information Centres.

February

GUILDFORD
Dicing for maid's money

April

MOLESEY
Children's Festival
Surrey Agricultural Show

May

CHARLWOOD
Charlwood Festival

ESHER
May Fair, Esher Green

FARNHAM
Southern Counties Craft Market,
The Maltings
Festival of Youth and Music

GODALMING
Surrey Show

KINGSTON-UPON-THAMES
Kingston-upon-Thames Festival

REIGATE
Reigate & Redhill Music Festival

RICHMOND
Richmond May Festival
Richmond Festival

TWICKENHAM
Twickenham Week

June

ABINGER HAMMER
Abinger Medieval Fair

BOXHILL
Music Festival

EPSOM
The Epsom Derby
Countryside Day, Norton Park

RICHMOND
Royal Horse Show, Old Deer Park

WALTON-ON-THAMES
Regatta

July

BYFLEET
Parish Day

EAST MOLESEY
55th Annual Metropolitan Horse Show & Tournament

EPSOM
Annual Fair

GUILDFORD
Guildford Festival

Events

HASLEMERE
Festival of Early Music

MERTON
Kite Festival, Mitcham Common

NEW MALDEN
Grand Market & Craft Fayre

TILFORD
Rustic Sunday, Old Kiln
Agricultural Museum

WOKING
Woking Whirl

August

EGHAM
Royal Show

MITCHAM
Mitcham Fair

THAMES DITTON
Metropolitan Police Dog
Championship

September

CHERTSEY
Chertsey Show

DORKING
Dorking Folk Festival

FARNBOFOUGH AIR SHOW
Farnborough Air Show

GUILDFORD SHOW
Guildford Show

KEW GARDENS
Annual Apron & Clog Race

October

CROYDON
Croydon Music Festival

FARNHAM
Southern Counties Craft Market

GODALMING
Surrey County Ploughing
Competition

GUILDFORD
Antiques Fair

KINGSTON-UPON-THAMES
Music Festival

November

SUTTON
Music Festival

WALTON/WEYBRIDGE
Round Table fireworks display

WOKING
Music Festival

Farm

This farm is a highly productive farm which offers visitors an opportunity to see how farm work is carried out. In addition to this farm listed below, many farms offer open days during the summer, so it is worthwhile checking with tourist information offices. When visiting a farm wear protective footwear and keep to marked paths.

LOSELEY HOUSE & FARM
Map 2 Ab
Guildford (0483) 571881
Loseley Park, Guildford
½m E Compton, ½m SW
Guildford off B3000
Open: early May-end Sep, Wed-Sat 14.00-17.00
Charge: 85p farm walks & ice cream, 90p (ch 85p) trailer rides, £1.10 (ch 65p) house, group reductions by arrangement
No dogs
Famous for its pedigree Jersey herd from which Loseley dairy produce is made, tours last about 1½ hours on foot (50 mins by trailer)
See also Historic Homes:
Loseley House

Field Study

JUNIPER HALL FIELD CENTRE /p19
Dorking (0306)
883849/87332
Dorking RH5 6DA
Juniper Hall is one of nine residential field centres in England and Wales run by the Field Studies Council. It organises courses throughout the year on natural history, conservation and geography. Visitors of all ages are welcome and courses are geared towards beginners and specialists. For further details write to the Warden and Director of Studies: J.E. Ebbington

Gardens

Surrey boasts many beautiful gardens which are open to the public. Many of them are owned by the National Trust or are attached to Historic Homes or Castles. Others are privately owned.

NATIONAL GARDENS SCHEME
(01) 730 0359
57 Lower Belgrave St, London
SW1W OLR
This charitable trust receives its funds from many gardens throughout England and Wales. Most of them are small, private gardens which open only a few times a year. Some larger gardens also contribute their takings on particular days. Money raised helps many causes, but particularly district nurses in need, either because of old age or illness or because of the stress and pressure of their work.

These gardens which support the scheme are indicated by the initials NGS.

It is not possible to list here all the gardens in Surrey which support the scheme since many of them are open only once a year. Included here are a selection of those open more often. The NGS publishes a booklet describing all the gardens in Surrey which support the scheme, as well as a booklet giving a complete list of all NGS gardens in England and Wales. To obtain copies of these booklets and for further information contact the address above.

BOHUNT MANOR
Map 2 Ba
Liphook (0428) 722208
Liphook, 3½m S Hindhead on A3
Open: all year, w/days, w/ends by arrangement, NGS open day last Sun in July, telephone in advance
Charge: 40p (ch 5p)
No dogs
🅿 ♿ 🍴

CHILWORTH MANOR
Map 2 Ac/p63
Guildford (0483) 61414
3½m SE Guildford off A248
Open: early April-late July, selected Weds & Sats 14.00-19.00, telephone in advance
Charge: 30p, 50p (garden & house)
🅿 ♿ 🍵🍴

CLANDON PARK
Formal gardens, most of the planting is recent with good displays of daffodils but the main park designed by Capability Brown is not open
See Historic Homes: Clandon Park
NT

CLAREMONT LANDSCAPE GARDEN
Map 3 Ba/p42
¼m S Esher E off A307
Open: April-end Oct, daily 9.00-19.00 (or dusk if earlier); Nov-end March 9.00-16.00 (closed 24 & 25 Dec, 1 Jan)
Charge: 50p (ch 25p)
Group tours (15) by arrangement with NT regional office (telephone Bookham 53401)
Dogs on leads
See also Historic Homes: Claremont
🅿 🍵

GORSE HILL MANOR
Map 1 Ab/p40
Wentworth (09904) 2101
Gorse Hill Rd, 1 m S Egham on
B380
Open: spring & autumn BHs,
14.00-17.30, other times &
groups by arrangement
Free (donations gratefully
accepted)
No dogs, no young children
NGS 🅿

GUILDFORD CASTLE
Map 2 Ab /p23
Castle ditch transformed into
flower garden seen at its best in
May
See Castles: Guildford Castle

HAMPTON COURT PALACE GARDENS
Map 3 Aa
East Molesey, 1 m E Sunbury on
A308
Open: all year, daily 8.00-dusk
Free
Replanted period gardens in
17th century style
See also Historic Homes:
Hampton Court Palace

HYDON NURSERIES
Map 2 Bb
Hascombe (048632) 252
Hydestile, 1½m SE Milford on
Milford to Hascombe Rd
Open: March-May & Oct-Nov,
Mon-Sat 8.30-17.00; June-Sep
& Dec-Feb, w/days 8.30-
17.00, Sat 8.30-13.00
Free
Plants for sale, dogs on lead
🅿 ﬕ

LONGHEATH
Map 3 Ba
Bookham (31) 53066
Burnhams Rd, Little Bookham,
4m SW Leatherhead off A246
Open: April-Oct by arrangement
only, NGS open day first Sun in
July
Charge: 30p (ch 15p)
Dogs on lead
NGS 🅿 ﬕ

OLD KILN AGRICULTURAL MUSEUM

10 acres including arboretum of woodland, planted with exotic and ornamental trees and shrubs
See also Museums: Old Kiln Agricultural Museum

PINEWOOD HOUSE
Map 1 Bb
(04867) 3241
Heath House Rd, Worplesdon Hill, 3½m SW Woking on A322
Open: May, Suns 14.00-18.00, other times by arrangement
Charge: 50p (ch 25p)
Plants for sale, no dogs or unaccompanied children
NGS ▣ ▱

POLESDEN LACY
Map 4 Aa
Great Bookham, 3m NW Dorking, 1½m S of town off A246
Open: all year, daily 11.00-dusk
Charge: 70p (ch 35p)
Edwardian style garden with lawns and fine trees underplanted with spring bulbs; lavender, iris, peony and rose garden linked by arched walkway
See also Historic Homes: Polesden Lacy
NT

RAMSTER
Map 2 Bb/p26
Chiddingfold, 4m S Godalming, ½m S Chiddingfold on A283
Open: late April-early June, w/ends 14.00-19.00, also May BH 14.00-19.00
Charge: 50p (ch & OAPs 30p)
NGS

ROYAL BOTANIC GARDENS
Map 3 Aa/p71
(01) 940 1171
Royal Botanic Gardens, Kew Rd, Richmond on A307
Open: all year, daily 10.00-20.00 (dusk if earlier), closed 25 Dec, 1 Jan
Charge: 25p (ch 10 free), school groups free w/days (write in advance)
No dogs
See also Historic Homes: Kew Palace & Queen Charlotte's Cottage
▣ ▤ ♿ ▱ ✕

SAVILL GARDENS
Map 1 Ab/p40
Windsor Great Park, 1½m SW Egham off A30 (access Wick Lane, Englefield Green)
Open: all year, daily 10.00-18.00 (closed 25 & 26 Dec)
Charge: £1.20 (ch16 free, OAPs £1.00), £1 each groups (20)
▣ ▤ ♿ ✕

STRAWBERRY HOUSE
Map 2 Bb
Haslemere (0428) 2613
Kingsley Green, 1m S Haslemere on A286
Open: telephone for details
Charge: 50p (ch 10p)
4 acres on Blackdown with flowering trees, shrubs, ornamental pond, waterfall, rockery and herbaceous borders
▣ ▱

SUTTON PLACE FARM
Map 2 Ac/p6
Abinger Hammer, 6m SW
Dorking on B2126
Open: last Sun in May & Aug,
14.00-18.00
Charge: 50p (ch 20p, cars
10p)
No dogs, plants for sale
NGS 🅿 ♿ ☕

SUTTON PLACE
Map 2 Ac/p63
Landscaped gardens by
Geoffrey Jellicoe, including
sculptural wall based on design
by Ben Nicholson, lake, surreal
and paradise gardens with rose
arbours, fountains and lily moat
See Art Galleries: Sutton Place

VALLEY GARDENS
Map 1 Ab
Windsor Great Park, 1 m S Savill
Gardens adjoining Virginia
Water lake
Open: all year, daily 8.30-dusk
Free (car park 70p)
Old redwoods, birches, coloured
conifers, maples, flowering
cherry trees, azaleas, magnolias
and rhododendrons
🅿

VANN
Map 2 Bb
Wormley (042879) 3413
Hambledon, 6m S Godalming
off A283
Open: Easter-end June,
telephone for details
Charge: 50p (ch 10p) open
days, £1 by arrangement
Dogs on leads, plant &
vegetables on sale
☕

WINKWORTH ARBORETEUM
Map 2 Bb/p53
Hascombe Rd, Godalming 3m
SE town off B2130
Open: all year, daily dawn-dusk
Charge: 50p (ch 25p)
Dogs on leads
Tea room & shop open selected
times
NT 🅿 ♿ ☕

WISLEY GARDENS
Map 1 Bc
Guildford (0483) 224234
2m NE Guildford on A3
Open: all year, daily 10.00-
19.00 (Sun 14.00-19.00) or
dusk, RHS members also Sun
10.00-14.00 (closed 25 Dec)
Charge: £1.30 (ch 65p),
groups (20) £1 (ch 55p), must
telephone & pay 14 days in
advance
No dogs, information centre,
plants for sale
🅿 ♿ ☕ ✕

YEW TREE COTTAGES
Map 3 Ba
(01) 398 3871
Esher, Portsmouth Rd, ½m from
town
Open: June, first & last Sun in
month 11.00-18.00, groups by
arrangement
Charge: 50p (ch 10p)
No dogs
NGS ☕

Golf Clubs

ADDINGTON COURT GOLF CLUB
Map 3 Bc
Croydon (01) 657 0281
Featherbed Lane, Addington, ½m W New Addington off A2202
18 holes (2)/parkland/5800 (5700) yds
9 holes/parkland/2300 yds
Par 68 (67)/SSS 68 (67)/pro
Visitors: anytime, public course
Charges: 18 holes £4.20 (£3.20), 9 holes £2.30, pitch & put £1

ADDINGTON PALACE GOLF CLUB
Map 3 Bc
Croydon (01) 654 3061
Gravel Hill, Addington, 1m E town off A212
18 holes/parkland/6262 yds
Par 71/SSS 71/pro
Visitors: anytime, w/ends with member only, must have handicap certificate
Charge: £10 without member, with member £5 w/days, £6 w/ends

BANSTEAD DOWNS GOLF CLUB
Map 3 Bb
(01) 642 2284
Burdon Lane, Belmont, Sutton W of A217
18 holes/downland/6150 yds
Par 69/SSS 69/pro
Visitors: anytime (Sat before 12.00 only), must telephone in advance
Charge: £8.50

BARROW HILLS GOLF CLUB
Map 1 Ab
Weybridge (97) 48117
Longcross, Chertsey 2½m W town off B386
18 holes/parkland/2957 yds
Par 56/SSS 56
Visitors: anytime with member only
Charge: telephone for details

BETCHWORTH PARK GOLF CLUB
Map 4 Aa
Dorking (0306) 882052
Reigate Rd, Dorking 1 m W
town off A25
18 holes/parkland/6250 yds
Par 70/SSS 70/pro
Visitors: anytime, telephone in
advance
Charge: w/days £8.50 per
day, £7.50 per round
🅿 🐾 ⛴ ✕ ⚲

BRAMLEY GOLF CLUB
Map 2 Ac
Guildford (0483) 892696
Gosden Hill, Bramley, Guildford,
2 m S town on A281
18 holes/slightly hilly
parkland/5910 yds
Par 68/SSS 68/pro
Visitors: anytime, w/ends with
member
Charge: £6 per round, £8 per
day
🅿 🐾 ⛴ ⚲

BURHILL GOLF CLUB
Map 3 Ba
Walton-on-Thames (09322)
27345
Walton-on-Thames, 1½m S of
town centre, W off B317 at
Hersham
18 holes/parkland/6213 yds
Par 70/SSS 70/pro
Visitors: anytime, must have
other club membership &
handicap certificate, w/ends
with introduction by member
only
Charges: £14 per day, £9 after
12.00
🅿 🐾 ⛴ ✕ ⚲

CAMBERLEY HEATH GOLF CLUB
Map 1 Bb
Camberley (0276) 23258
Portsmouth Rd, Camberley, 1 m
E town on A325
18 holes/heathland/6402 yds
Par 72/SSS 71/pro
Visitors: must have letter of
introduction from own club
Charge: £8.50 per round,
£12.50 per day
🅿 🐾 ⛴ ✕ ⚲

CHIPSTEAD GOLF CLUB
Map 3 Bb
Downland (07375) 55781
How Lane, Coulsdon, 1 m SW
Purley
18 holes/parkland/5407 yds
Par 67/SSS 66
ro
Visitors: anytime, w/ends with
member only
Charge: £7 per round
🅿 🐾 ⛴ ⚲

COOMBE HILL GOLF CLUB
Map 3 Aa
(01) 942 2284
Golf Club Drive, Kingston Hill,
1 m NE Kingston on A238
18 holes/hilly/6256 yds
Par 70/SSS 71/pro
Visitors: anytime, must have
other club membership &
handicap certificate
Charge: w/days £12, w/ends
£15
🅿 🐾 ⛴ ✕ ⚲

CROHAM HURST GOLF CLUB
Map 3 Bb
(01) 6578 2075
Croham Rd, South Croydon, off
B275
18 holes/parkland/6234 yds
Par 70/SSS 70/pro
Visitors: anytime, must
telephone in advance
Charge: £12 per day
🅿 🍴 🍺

CUDDINGTON GOLF CLUB
Map 3 Bb
(01) 393 0952
Banstead Rd, Banstead, 150
yds from station off B2032
18 holes/parkland/6300 yds
Par 70/SSS 70/pro
Visitors: anytime (telephone in
advance), must have other club
membership & handicap
certificate
Charge: w/days £9 per day,
w/ends £12 per day
🅿 🍴 🍺🍽🍷

DORKING GOLF CLUB
Map 4 Aa
Dorking (0306) 886917
Chart Park, Dorking, S town off
A24
9 holes/undulating
parkland/5120 yds
Par 66/SSS 65/pro
Visitors: anytime, handicap
certificate preferred but not
essential
Charge: £5 per day, £3 with
member
🅿 🍴 🍺 🍷

DRIFT GOLF & COUNTRY CLUB
Map 2 Ac
East Horsley (04865) 4641
The Drift, East Horsley, 2½m S
A3 off B2039
18 holes/woodland/6500 yds
Par 72/SSS 71/pro
Visitors: w/days only, advisable
to telephone in advance
Charge: £6 per round, £8 per
day
🅿 🍴 🍺🍽🍷

EFFINGHAM GOLF CLUB
Map 4 Aa
Bookham (31) 52203
Guildford Rd, Effingham, 8m E
Guildford on A246
18 holes/downland/6488 yds
Par 71/SSS 71/pro
Visitors: w/days only,
telephone in advance
Charge: £10 per day, £7 after
12.00
🅿 🍴 🍺🍽🍷

EPSOM & EWELL GOLF CLUB
Map 3 Ba
Epsom (78) 23363
Longdown Lane, South Epsom,
300 yds Epsom Downs Station
on A241
18 holes/downland/5711 yds
Par 69/SSS 68/pro
Visitors: w/days except Tue
mornings, w/ends after 11.00,
advisable to telephone in
advance
Charge: £4.50 per day
🅿 🍴 🍺 🍷

FARNHAM GOLF CLUB
Map 2 Aa
Runfold (02518) 2109
The Sands, Farnham, 1½m E
town off A31
18 holes/parkland, pine &
heath/6221 yds
Par 72/SSS 70/pro
Visitors: anytime, must have
other club membership &
handicap certificate
Charge: £8.50 per day, £6.50
per round
🅿 🈂 ⛁✕ ♀

FOXHILLS GOLF & COUNTRY CLUB
Map 1 Bc
Ottershaw (093287) 2050
Stonehill Rd, Ottershaw, l½m N
town off A320
18 holes(2)
parkland(woodland)
6658 (6406) yds
Par 72(71)/SSS 72(71)
Visitors: anytime
Charge: w/days £8 per round,
£11 per day, w/ends £12 per
day
🅿 🈂 ⛁✕ ♀

GATTON MANOR HOTEL & GOLF CLUB
Map 4 Ba
Oakwood Hill (030679) 555/6
Ockley, Dorking, 6m S town off
A29
18 holes/flat,
challenging/6906 yds
Par 72/SSS 72/pro
Visitors: Mon-Sat, after 12.00
Sun
Charge: w/days £8 per day, £5
per round, w/ends £10 per day,
£6 per round
🅿 🈂 ⛁✕ ♀

GUILDFORD GOLF CLUB
Map 2 Ac
Guildford (0483) 575243
High Path Rd, Merrow, 1½m E
Guildford off A246
18 holes/downland/6100 yds
Par 69/SSS 70/pro
Visitors: Mon-Fri, Sun
afternoon
Charge: £8 per day, £5 per
round, £6 Sun
🅿 🈂 ⛁✕ ♀

HANKLEY COMMON GOLF CLUB
Map 2 Bb
Frensham (025125) 2493
South Tilford, 3m SE Farnham
off A287
18 holes/heathland/6403 yds
Par 71/SSS 71/pro
Visitors: anytime, w/ends
telephone in advance, must
have other club membership &
handicap certificate
Charge: w/days £10 per day,
w/ends £12 per day
🅿 🈂 ⛁✕ ♀

HINDHEAD GOLF CLUB
Map 2 Ba
Hindhead (042873) 4614
Churt Rd, Hindhead, 1½m NW
town on A287
18 holes/heath &
heather/6349 yds
Par 70/SSS 70/pro
Visitors: anytime, must
telephone in advance
Charge: w/days £9, W/ends &
BHs £12
🅿 🈂 ⛁✕ ♀

HOME PARK GOLF CLUB
Map 3 Aa
(01) 977 2423
Hampton Wick, Kingston upon
Thames, S Hampton Wick in
Hampton Court Park 1 3/4m
Kingston Bridge
18 holes/parkland/6496 yds
Par 71/SSS 71/pro
Visitors: anytime, must
telephone in advance
Charge: w/days £5 per round,
w/ends £6 per round
🅿 ⚑ 🍽️ ♀

KINGSWOOD GOLF CLUB
Map 3 Bb
Mogador (0737) 832188
Sandy Lane, Kingswood, 6m S
Sutton off A217
18 holes/parkland/6821 yds
Par 73/SSS 73/pro
Visitors: anytime by prior
arrangement
Charge: w/days before 13.00
£9.50, 13.00-16.00 £7.50,
after 16.00 £4.50
Four squash courts
🅿 ⚑ 🍽️ ♀

LALEHAM GOLF CLUB
Map 1 Ac
Chertsey (09328) 64211
Laleham Reach, 1m N Chertsey
off A320
18 holes/well bunkered
parkland/meadowland/6203
yds
Par 70/SSS 70/pro
Visitors: anytime, w/ends with
member only
Charge: £6 per round, £8 per
day
🅿 ⚑ 🍽️ ♀

LEATHERHEAD GOLF CLUB
Map 3 Ba
Leatherhead (0372) 372013
Oxshott Rd, Leatherhead, 1½m
N town on A244
18 holes/parkland/6100 yds
Par 70/SSS 70/pro
Visitors: by arrangement only
Charge: £8 per day, £10 per
round
🅿 ⚑ 🍽️ ♀

LIMPSFIELD CHART GOLF CLUB
Map 4 Ac
Limpsfield (088388) 2106
Limpsfield, Nr Oxted, 1m W
Limpsfield on A25
9 holes/heathland/5233 yds
Par 70/SSS 68/pro
Visitors: w/days, Thu after
14.30, w/ends telephone in
advance
Charge: w/days £5 (£2.50
with member), w/ends £8 (£4
with member)
🅿 ⚑ 🍽️ ♀

MITCHAM GOLF CLUB
Map 3 Ab
(01) 648 4197
Carshalton Rd, Mitcham
Junction, 1m E Mitcham off
A236
18 holes/heathland/5931 yds
Par 69/SSS 68/pro
Visitors: anytime, subject to
restrictions at w/ends
Charge: w/days £3 per round,
w/ends £4 per round
🅿 ⚑ 🍽️ ♀

MOORE PLACE GOLF CLUB
Map 3 Ba
Esher (78) 63533
Portsmouth Rd, Esher 1 m SW
town on A3
9 holes/undulating
parkland/2049 yds
Par 32/SSS 30/pro
Visitors: anytime (public
course)
Charge: w/days £1.40,
w/ends £1.90
🅿 🥤 ⌂ ✕ ♇

NEW ZEALAND GOLF CLUB
Map 1 Bc
Byfleet (91) 45049
Woodham Lane, Weybridge,
1 m NW of West Byfleet Station
on A245
18 holes/heathland/6012 yds
Par 69/SSS 69/pro
Visitors: w/days only, must
have other club membership &
handicap certificate
Charge: £10.50 per day
🅿 🥤 ⌂ ✕ ♇

NORTH DOWNS GOLF CLUB
Map 3 Bc
Woldingham (905)
3298/2057
Northdown Rd, Woldingham,
3 m N Caterham off A22
18 holes/downland/5761
yds
Par 68/SSS 68/pro
Visitors: anytime
Charge: Apr-Oct £9 per day
(£7 after 14.30), Nov-Mar £7
per day
🅿 🥤 ⌂ ✕ ♇

OAKS PARK SPORTS CENTRE
Map 3 Bb
(01) 643 8363
Woodmansterne Rd, Carshalton,
4½m S town W off B278
18 (9) holes /parkland/5873
yds
Par 70/SSS 70/pro
Visitors: anytime
Charge: w/days £3, w/ends
£4
🅿 🥤 ⌂ ✕ ♇

R.A.C. COUNTRY CLUB
Map 3 Ba
Woodcote Park, Wilmerehatch
Lane, Epsom, 2½m S town off
A24
18 holes (2)/picturesque
parkland/6672 (5520) yds
Par 72(67)/SSS 72(67)/pro
Visitors: anytime with
member,w/ends & BHs only
one visitor per member allowed
🅿 🥤 ⌂ ✕ ♇

REDHILL & REIGATE GOLF CLUB
Map 4 Ab
Reigate (74) 44433
Earlswood Common, Redhill,
1 m S town on A23
18 holes/parkland/5193 yds
Par 67/SSS 65/pro
Visitors: anytime
Charge: w/days £3, w/ends
£5
🅿 🥤 ⌂ ♇

REIGATE HEATH GOLF CLUB
Map 4 Ab
Reigate (74) 42610
Flanchford Rd, Reigate, S of
A25 on W of town
9 holes/heathland/5554 yds
Par 67/SSS 67
Visitors: by arrangement only
Charge: £7 per day, £5.50 per
round
🅿 🍴 🖵✕ ♀

ROYAL MID-SURREY GOLF
CLUB
Map 3 Aa
(01) 940 1894
Old Deer Park, Richmond, on
A316
18 holes (2)/parkland/6331
(5544) yds
Par 69/SSS 70(67)/pro
Visitors: w/days, must be
member of recognised club and
have handicap certificate,
w/ends with member only
Charge: £12 per day
🅿 🍴 🖵✕ ♀

ST GEORGES HILL GOLF
CLUB
Map 1 Bc
Weybridge (0932) 42406
St Georges Hill, Weybridge ½m
S town off B374
2 courses: 18 holes private (9
holes public)
18 (9) holes/undulating
woodland/6473 (2706) yds
Par 71(35)/SSS 71(35)/pro
Visitors: anytime by letter of
introduction only, (public course,
no clubhouse facilities)
🅿 🍴 🖵✕ ♀(18 only)

SANDOWN PARK GOLF
COURSE & GOLF CENTRE
Map 3 Ba
Esher (0372) 659201/63340
Sandown Park Racecourse,
More Lane, Esher, W off A3
Pitch & Putt and par 3 course
9 hole/parkland/5658 yds
Par 70/SSS 67/pro
Visitors: w/days, restricted
w/ends & BHs
Charge: £2 w/days, £2.60
w/ends; Pitch & Putt 90p; par
3 course £1.30 w/days, £1.50
w/ends
Indoor driving range
🅿 🍴 🖵 ♀

SHIRLEY PARK GOLF CLUB
Map 3 Ba
01-654 1143
Addiscombe Rd, Croydon on
A232 1m E Croydon Station
18 holes/parkland/6210 yds
Par 71/SSS 71/pro
Visitors: w/days, telephone in
advance; w/end with member
only
Charge: £11 per round, per day
🅿 🍴 🖵✕ ♀

SILVERMERE GOLF CLUB
Map 3 Ba
Cobham (09326) 6007
Cobham, 3m W town off A245
18 holes/9 heathland, 9
parkland meadows/6704 yds
Par 73/SSS 72/pro
Visitors: anytime
Charge: w/days £4, w/ends
£5, ½ price twilight ticket
🅿 🍴 🖵✕ ♀

SUNNINGDALE GOLF CLUB
Map 1 Ab
Ascot (0990) 21681
18 holes(2)/heatherland/6601
(6336) yds
Par 71(69)/SSS 71(69)/pro
Visitors: anytime, by
arrangement only and must
have letter of introduction
Charge: £17 per day
🅿 🍴 ☕ ✕ ⚲

SURBITON GOLF CLUB
Map 3 Ba
(01) 398 3101
Woodstock Lane, Chessington,
off A3
18 holes/parkland/6211 yds
Par 70/SSS 70/pro
Visitors: anytime, w/ends with
member only
Charge: £9.50 per day
🅿 🍴 ☕ ✕ ⚲

TANDRIDGE GOLF CLUB
Map 4 Ac
Oxted (08833) 2273/4
Tandridge, Oxted, 1 m W Oxted
off A25
18 holes/parkland/6260 yds
Par 69/SSS 70/pro
Visitors: Mon, Wed & Thur by
arrangement only
Charge: £11.50 per day,
£9.50 after 13.00, £7 with
member
🅿 🍴 ☕ ✕ ⚲

**THAMES DITTON & ESHER
GOLF CLUB**
Map 3 Ba
(01) 398 1551
Marquis of Granby, Portsmouth
Rd, Esher, E town off A307
9 holes/commonland without
bunkers/5190 yds
Par 66/SSS 64/pro

Visitors: Mon-Sat; Sun before
12.00
Charge: w/days £2.50,
w/ends £3.50
🅿 🍴 ☕ ⚲

TYRELLS WOOD GOLF CLUB
Map 3 Ba
Leatherhead (03723) 76025
Tyrells Wood Estate,
Leatherhead, SW town off
B2033
18 holes/rolling hills/6022 yds
Par 69/SSS 69/pro
Visitors: w/days, w/ends after
12.00, must telephone in
advance
Charge: w/days £8.50,
w/ends & BHs £12
🅿 🍴 ☕ ✕ ⚲

WALTON HEATH GOLF CLUB
Map 3 Bb
Tadworth (037781) 2380
Tadworth, 1 m S town on
B2032
18 holes(2)/heathland/6813
(6659) yds
Par 73(72)/SSS 73(72)/pro
Visitors: w/days by
arrangement only
Charge: £14 per day, £10 after
11.30
🅿 🍴 ☕ ✕ ⚲

**WENTWORTH GOLF CLUB
LTD**
Map 1 Ab
Wentworth (09904) 2201
Virginia Water, signposted on
A30 adjacent to Wheatsheaf
Hotel
International championship
course (East Course) in Burma
Rd
18 holes(2)/heathland &
parkland/6945 (East Course
6176) yds
Par 72(68)/SSS 74(70)/pro

Visitors: by arrangement only, must have membership of recognised club & handicap certificate
Charge: £15 per day
🅿 🥾 ✕ ♀

WEST BYFLEET GOLF CLUB LTD
Map 1 Bc
Byfleet (91) 45230
Sheerwater Rd, West Byfleet, off A245
18 holes/tree-lined/6211 yds
Par 70/SSS 70/pro
Visitors: w/days, must have membership of recognised club & handicap certificate; w/ends with member only
Charge: £9.50 per day
🅿 🥾 ✕ ♀

WEST HILL GOLF CLUB
Map 1 Bb
Brookwood (04867) 2110/4365
West Hill, Brookwood, 3m W Woking off A322
18 holes/parkland/6407 yds
Par 71/SSS 71/pro
Visitors: by arrangment only, must have membership of recognised club & handicap certificate
Charge: w/days £9 per round, £13 per day; w/ends £12 per round, £24 per day
🅿 🥾 ✕ ♀

WEST SURREY GOLF CLUB
Map 2 Bb
Godalming (04868) 21275
Enton Green, Godalming, 2½m S town off A3100
18 hole/parkland/6235 yds
Par 71/SSS 70/pro

Visitors: w/days, by arrangement only, must have other club membership & handicap certificate
Charge: £10 per day, after 13.00 £7.50
🅿 🥾 ⛾ ✕ ♀

WORPLESDON GOLF CLUB
Map 1 Bb
Brookwood (04867) 2277
Heath House Rd, Woking, 2m town
18 holes/heatherland/6422 yds
Par 71/SSS 71/pro
Visitors: w/days, must telephone in advance, must have other club membership & handicap certificate; w/ends with member only
Charge: £13 per round, £9 per day
🅿 🥾 ⛾ ✕ ♀

Greyhound Racing

ALDERSHOT STADIUM
Map 2 Ab
Aldershot (0252) 20182
Oxendon Rd, Tongham ½m NE
Farnham off A3014
Open: all year, Wed & Fri
19.30-21.30
Charge: £2.50 (ch £1); group
(10) reductions by arrangement
See also Motor Racing:
Aldershot Stadium
🅿 ♿ 🍺 ♀

Gymnastics

AMATEUR GYMNASTICS ASSOCIATION
c/o The Sports Council, Greater
London & SE Region
01-580 9092/7
160 Great Portland St, London
W1 5TB
This is the governing body for
the sport in Britain. The
following clubs are affiliated to
the Association.

CAMBERLEY G.C.
Secretary: Mrs Bernie Wright
Camberley (0276)
61926/21624
ll Holly Hedge Close, Frimley

COBHAM G.C.
Secretary: Mrs D Older
(01) 398 1883
58 Longmead Rd, Thames
Ditton

CONNAUGHT G.C.
Secretary: Mrs Frances Quirk
Bagshot (0276) 72853
37 Grasmere Rd, Lightwater

GUILDFORD G.C.
Secretary: Mrs E Dean
Guildford (0483) 65106
Lentrain, Roseacre Gardens,
Chilworth

LEATHERHEAD G.C.
Secretary: Mrs Margaret Miler
Horley (029 34) 73224
61 Avondale Close, Horley

PYRFORD G.C.
Secretary: Mrs P Stancel
Brookwood (048 67) 81304
2 Robins Dale, Knaphill

ST MAUR'S CONVENT
Secretary: Sue Miller
Weybridge (97) 51411
16 Camden Cottages, Church
Walk, Weybridge

SPELTHORNE G.C.
Secretary: Miss J Starkings
Ashford (69) 55370
396 London Rd, Ashford

WOKING G.C.
Secretary: Mrs P Stancel
Brookwood (04867) 81304
2 Robins Dale, Knaphill

Historic Homes

ALBURY PARK
Map 2 Ac /p49
Shere (048641) 2964
Albury, 1 m E Guildford off
A25/A248
Open: May-Sep, Wed & Thur
14.00-16.00
Charge: 50p (ch 25p)
No dogs
🅿

CHILWORTH MANOR
See Gardens: Chilworth Manor

CLANDON PARK
Map 2 Ac /p35
West Clandon, 3m NE Guildford
on A246
Open: April-mid Oct, Tues-
Thurs, w/end & BHs 14.00-
18.00 (last admission 17.30)
Charge: £1.40 (ch 70p), group
reductions by arrangement
Dogs on leads
See also Gardens: Clandon
Park
See also Museums: Queen's
Royal Surrey Regiment Museum
NT 🅿 ⚓ ♿ ⌖ ✕

CLAREMONT
Map 3 Ba /p42
Esher (0372) 67841
Claremont Drive, ¼m S Esher
on A244
Open: Feb-Nov, first w/end in
month

Charge: 75p (ch, OAPs 35p),
group reductions (10) by
arrangement
See also Gardens: Claremont
Garden
No dogs
🅿 ♿ �—

DETILLENS
Map 4 Ac /p80
Oxted (08833) 3342
Limpsfield, E town on B269
Open: May-end June, Sat
14.00-17.00; July-Sep, Wed &
Sat 14.00-17.00; BHs
Group tours by arrangement
Charge: £1.25 (ch 60p)
No dogs
🅿

GREATHED MANOR
Map 4 Bc
Lingfield (0342) 832577
Dormansland, 2m SE Lingfield,
1m S of B2028
Open: May-Sep, Wed & Thur
14.00-17.00
Charge: 50p (ch 25p)
No dogs
🅿 ♿

GUILDFORD HOUSE
See Art Galleries: Guildford
House

HAM HOUSE
Map 3 Aa /p88
Ham, Richmond on A307
Open: April-end Sep, Tues-Sun
14.00-18.00; Oct-end March,
Tues-Sun 12.00-16.00 (last
admission half hour before
closing); BHs (closed Good Fri,
May BH, 25 & 26 Dec & 1
Jan)

Charge: £1, reductions for ch, OAPs & groups by arrangement Ch must be accompanied by adult; guided tours by arrangement with Dept of Education, Victoria & Albert Museum, London SW7
NT ▣ ▐▄ ✆

HAMPTON COURT PALACE
Map 3 Aa /p76
1 m NW Kingston, 1 m N Hampton Wick off A308
Open: April-Sep, Mon-Sat 9.30-18.00 (Sun 11.00-18.00); Oct-March 9.30-17.00 (Sun 14.00-17.00)
Charge: £1.80 (ch 90p) April-Sep; 90p (ch 50p) Oct-March; school reductions by arrangement with superintendent; group reductions (11)
Guided tours
See also Gardens: Hampton Court
▣ ▐▄ ✆ ✕

HATCHLANDS
Map 2 Ac/P34
East Clandon, 2 m NE Guildford on A246
Open: April-mid Oct, Wed, Thur & Sun 14.00-18.00 (last admission 17.30)
Charge: 80p (ch 40p)
NT ✆

KEW PALACE (DUTCH HOUSE)
Map 3 Aa /p72
Kew Gardens, Kew off A307
Open: April-Oct, daily 11.00-17.30
Charge: 60p (ch & OAPs 30p)
See also Gardens: Royal Botanic Gardens

LOSELEY HOUSE
Map 2 Ab /p63
Loseley Park, 1 m SW Guildford off B3000
Elegant 16th century mansion in Bargate stone with fine ceilings, carved chalk chimneys, collections of furniture, tapestry & needlework
See also Farms: Loseley House and Farm

OLD PALACE
Map 3 Bb /p29
(01) 680 5877/6882027
Old Palace Rd, Croydon
Open: Easter BH (except Mon), summer BH, last two weeks July, telephone for details
Charge: £1 (ch & OAPs 75p)
▣ ▐▄ ✆

PINEWOOD HOUSE
See also Gardens: Pinewood House

POLESDEN LACEY
Map 4 Aa
Great Bookham, 3m NW Dorking, 1½m S town off A246
Open: March & Nov, w/ends 14.00-17.00; April-Oct, Tue-Thur, w/end & BHs 14.00-18.00 (closed Good Fri)
Charge: 90p (ch 45p); £1.30 (ch 75p) house & garden; group reductions by arrangement
No dogs, prams or pushchairs
See also Gardens: Polesden Lacy
NT ▐▄ ✕

QUEEN CHARLOTTE'S COTTAGE
Map 3 Aa /p72
Kew Gardens, Kew off A307
Open: April-mid Oct, w/ends &
BH Mons 11.00-17.30
Charge: 30p (ch16 & OAPs
15p)
Built 1772 for the Queen and
used by the family as summer
house; interior remains as it was
in the 18th century when
royalty lived there
See also Gardens: Royal
Botanic Gardens

SUTTON PLACE
Map 2 Ac
Guildford
Build in 16th century by Sir
Richard Weston, fine example of
early Renaissance architecture
See Gardens: Sutton Place
See Art Galleries: Sutton Place

THE CEDARS
See Museums: Chertsey
Museum

TITSEY PLACE
See Woodlands: Titsey
Plantation

WILLMER HOUSE
See Museums: Farnham
Museum

Horseracing

EPSOM DOWNS RACECOURSE
Map 3 Bb /p40
Epsom (03727) 26311
½m S Epsom on B290
Open: 9 days per year; April (3
days), June (4 days), Aug BH
Mon & Tue
Charge: £7.50 (club enclosure),
£4.50 (paddock)
Flat racing only
🅿 🍴 ⛴ ✗ ♀

KEMPTON RACECOURSE
Map 3 Aa
Sunbury (76) 82292
N of Sunbury town centre on
A308
Open: 19 meetings a year,
May-Dec (telephone for details)
Charge: £7.50 (day
membership), £10 (features
day), £4.50 (grandstand);
discounts for groups by
arrangement
National Hunt & flat racing
P ⊒✗♀

SANDOWN PARK
RACECOURSE
Map 3 Ba/p42
Esher (78) 63072
½m N Esher off A244
Open: 25 meetings a year,
May-Dec
Charge: £7.50 (daily
membership), £10 (feature
days), £4.50 grandstand;
discount for groups by
arrangement
National Hunt and flat racing
P ⊒✗♀

LINGFIELD PARK
RACECOURSE
Map 4 Bc/p81
Lingfield (0342) 832009
½m S Lingfield off B2028
Open: 26 meetings a year,
May-Dec
Charge: £7 (ch £2) club
enclosure, £4 grandstand (ch16
free, OAPs £2.50), £2.50 picnic
area (car occupants), £1 car
park
Private boxes available,
telephone for details; group
discounts by arrangement with
promotions executive
Country course with full tote
facilities
P ⊒⊞✗♀

Ice Skating

RICHMOND ICE RINK
Map 3 Aa
(01) 892 3646
Clevedon Rd, Twickenham
Open: all year, 3 sessions daily,
10.00-12.30, 14.30-17.00
&19.30-22.00 (closed 25 &
26 Dec)
Charge: w/days £1.20 (ch
90p), w/ends £1.40 (ch 90p),
skate hire 50p
Venue for Richmond Trophy, an
international competition for
women; also the British Figure
Skating Championships in mid
November; Ice Fayre including
ice carnival, figure skating,
curling and dance exhibitions
(telephone for details)
P ⛸ ⊒♀

Markets

Markets are an important aspect of rural life and Surrey's towns offer a wide variety including traditional cattle markets. It is still possible to buy fresh fruit and vegetables from the farms as well as homemade jams and preserves in season. Antique markets are plentiful as are more general markets selling an enormously wide range of goods from street stalls.

Go early if you want to buy fresh produce or catch a real bargain.

Markets which are labelled General, WI or Livestock are explained below, other descriptions, such as Antiques, are self explanatory.

GENERAL
General markets offer a wide range of inexpensive new goods from clothing and bedding to jewellery and china; in addition many of these markets also sell fresh food including meat and vegetables and have stalls selling such things as sweets and cosmetics.

WI
Womens Institute markets are run by members of the institute and usually sell home made foods such as jams and cakes and other home produces products.

LIVESTOCK
These are the markets to which farmers bring their sheep, cattle and other animals for selling and to buy livestock through auctions.

BANSTEAD
WI: Fri 10.30-12.00, The Lady Neville Pavilion, Avenue Rd

BOOKHAM
WI: Fri 10.15-11.30, Barn Hall, Church Rd

CHERTSEY
General: Sat 7.00-15.00, Windsor St

CHIDDINGFOLD
WI: Fri 10.00-11.30, Cedar Hall, Coxcombe Lane

CHOBHAM
WI: Thur 9.30-11.30, Village Hall, Woking Rd

CRANLEIGH
General: Thur 9.30-11.30, Recreation Centre car park
WI: Thur 10.30-12.00, The Guide Hall, Village Way

DORKING
WI: Fri 9.45-11.30, Mulberry Centre, Junction Rd
General: Fri 7.30-17.30, off High St
Crafts: Sat 8.30-16.30, off High St

EPSOM
General: Tue, Fri & Sat 8.00-17.30, High St

FARNHAM
WI: Fri 9.00-12.00, Castle St
Antiques: once a month, The Maltings Market

GODALMING
WI: Fri 8.30-10.30, United Church Hall, Bridge St
General: Fri 9.00-16.00, Moss Lane

GUILDFORD
Crafts: June-Sep, Sat 9.00-16.00, Old Town Bridge
Fruit & Veg: Fri & Sat, 7.00-17.45 North St
Cattle: Tue 8.00-14.00, Slyfield Green
General: Wed 8.00-16.00, Slyfield Green
Cars: once a month, Slyfield Green

HASLEMERE
Museum Market: once a month, Haslemere Hall

HORLEY
WI: Fri 10.30-12.00, Methodist Church Hall, Victoria Rd

LEATHERHEAD
WI: Fri 10.30-11.30, The Parish Hall

OXTED
WI: Thur 10.30-11.45, Red Cross Centre, station car park

REDHILL
General: Sat & Thur 9.00-17.00, Ladbroke Rd

REIGATE
WI: Fri 9.30-11.30, Methodist Church School Room, High St

WOKING
General: Tue, Fri & Sat 9.30-16.00, Market Square

Mills

ELSTEAD MILL
Map 2 Ab
Elstead (0252) 703132
Farnham Rd, Elstead on B3001
Open: now a restaurant but can be viewed anytime from exterior Brick Georgian building listed grade 2 with cupola housing a bell that once summoned people to work; retains 18th century wheel on site of mill dating back to the Conquest; converted in early 1880s to paper production

GOMSHALL MILL & GALLERY
Map 2 Ac
Shere (048641) 2433
Gomshall, 2m W Dorking on A25
Open: all year, Tue-Sun & BHs 10.00-17.30
Historic watermill on River Tillingbourne, now a restaurant, art gallery & craft shop; original water wheel survives and old mill race visible through glass from restaurant
See also Crafts: Gomshall Mill Pottery
🅿 🕿 ♿ ✗

175

HAXTED WATERMILL
See Museums: The Watermill Museum

REIGATE HEATH WINDMILL
Map 4 Ab
Flanchford Rd, Reigate Heath, ½m W Reigate off A25
Open: May-Oct, 3rd Sun in month 15.00 (church services); other time by arrangement with caretaker in adjoining cottage
Free
Old windmill converted to church, restored to original appearance but not in working order

SHALFORD MILL
Map 2 Ac/p64
Shalford, 1½m SE Guildford on S side of A281
Open: all year, daily by application to 45, The Street, Shalford
Free
Early 18th century watermill, part of which is now a private residence but the rest can be viewed and consists of timber storeys, original machinery, the mill wheel & stone
Children must be accompanied
NT

WRAY COMMON WINDMILL
Wray Common, ½m NW Reigate
Not open to public but visible from the exterior anytime; tower mill complete with cap, gallery and fantail staging; now a private residence

Motor Racing

ALDERSHOT STADIUM
Map 2 Ab
Aldershot (0252) 20182
Oxenden Rd, Tongham, 1½m NE Farnham off A3014
Open: all year, Thurs 19.30-23.00

Charge: £2.50 (ch £1); group (10) reductions by arrangement
Formula racing, also greyhound racing **See Greyhound Racing**
Aldershot Stadium
🅿 ♿ ⛺ 🍴

Museums

AIRBORNE FORCES MUSEUM
Map 2 Aa
Aldershot (0252) 24431 Ext 619
Parachute Regiment Depot, Browning Barracks, Queens Avenue, Aldershot
Open: all year, (closed Dec 25) Mon-Sat 9.00-12.30 & 14.00-16.30; Sun 10.00-12.30 & 14.00-16.30
Charge;25p (ch & Service Members 15p)
No dogs
🅿 🅿 ♿

BOURNE HALL MUSEUM
Map 3 Bb /p45
(01) 393 9573
Bourne Hall, Spring Street, Ewell
Open: all year, Mon, Wed & Thur 10.00-20.00, Tue & Fri 10.00-20.00, Sat 9.30-17.00 (closed Dec 25, Jan 1 & BHs)
Free
Publications available, no dogs
🅿 ♿ ⛺

THE BROOKING COLLECTION
Map 2 Ab /p62
Guildford (0483) 504555
Woodhay, White Hart Lane, Guildford
Open: all year, w/ends only (must telephone in advance)
Charge: £1

BUS MUSEUM
Map 3 Ba
Cobham (266) 4078
Redhill Rd, Cobham
Open: last Sun in every month (telephone in advance), open day 2nd Sun in April
Free (donations gratefully accepted)
🅿

CHERTSEY MUSEUM
Map 1 Ac
Chertsey (09328) 65764
The Cedars, 33 Windsor Street, Chertsey
Open: all year, Tue & Thur 14.00-17.00, Wed, Fri & Sat 10.00-13.00 & 14.00-17.00 (closed BHs)
Free
Group tours of reserve stock by arrangement with curator, no dogs
🅿 ♿

DORKING MUSEUM
Map 4 Aa/p33
Dorking (0306) 883429
West St, Dorking
Open: all year, Wed, Thur 14.00-17.00, Sat 10.00-17.00
Charge: 10p (ch 5p)
🅿

CATERHAM MUSEUM
Map 3 Bb
Caterham (0883) 40275
1 Stafford Rd, Caterham Town
Centre
Open: all year, Wed & Sat
10.00-17.00, Sun 14.00-
17.00 (closed Dec 25 & 26)
Charge: 20p (ch & OAP 10p)
Groups by arrangement
No dogs
🐾 ♿ ☕

EDUCATIONAL MUSEUM
Map 2 Bb
Haslemere (0428) 2112
High St, Haslemere
Open: Easter-end Sep, Tue-Sat
10.00-17.00, Sun 14.00-
17.00; early Nov-end Mar, Tue-
Sat 10.00-16.00
Charge: 45p (ch 20p),
membership available £3.50
annual, £50 life
Groups by arrangement
No dogs, no smoking
🅿 🐾

EGHAM MUSEUM
Map 1 Ac
Egham (87) 36645
Literary Institute, High St,
Egham
Open: all year, Sat 10.30-
12.30 & 14.30-16.30, Thur
14.00-16.00
Free
No dogs
🅿 🐾

FARNHAM MUSEUM
Map 2 Aa
Farnham (0252) 715094
Willmer House, 38 West St,
Farnham
Open: all year, Tue-Sat 11.00-
17.00; also Weds (May-Sep)
19.00-21.00; BH Mons 14.00-
17.00 (closed 25 & 26 Dec)
Free
Dogs on leads
🅿 🐾 ♿

GODALMING MUSEUM
Map 2 Ab /p51
Godalming (04868) 4104
The Old Town Hall, High St,
Godalming
Open: all year, Tues-Sat 15.00-
17.00 (closed BHs, 25 & 26
Dec)
Free
Dogs on leads
🐾

**GORDON BOY'S SCHOOL
MUSEUM**
Map 1 Bb
Chobham (09905) 8084
West End 15, 5m NE Woking
on A322
Open: during school term by
arrangement only
Free (donations gratefully
accepted)
No dogs
🅿

GUILDFORD MUSEUM
Map 2 Bb /p61
Guildford (0453) 66551
Castle Arch, Guildford
Open: all year, Mon-Sat 11.00-
17.00
Free
Disabled people by arrangement
No dogs, no smoking
🐾 ♿

HOLMESDALE NATURAL HISTORY CLUB MUSEUM
Map 4 Ab
Reigate (74) 46574
14 Croydon Rd, Croydon
Open: selected days during spring BH, telephone in advance
Free
Membership: £3 single, £4.50 double (includes use of library & museum, lectures, nature walks)
For information telephone Mon afternoons

KINGSTON MUSEUM & HERITAGE CENTRE
Map 3 Aa /p75
(01) 546 5386
Fairfield Way, Kingston upon Thames
Open: all year, Mon-Sat 10.00-17.00 (closed BHs)
Free
Groups welcome by arrangement
No dogs
🅿 ♿ ⛪

LEATHERHEAD MUSEUM
Map 3 Ba /p78
Bookham (31) 58722
Hampton Cottage, 65 Church St, Leatherhead
Open: April-Dec, Sat 10.00-16.00, Fri 10.00-13.00; groups at other times by arrangement with Mr David Bruce, Curator
Free (donations gratefully accepted)
No dogs
🅿 ♿ ⛪

MUSEUM OF COUNTRY CRAFTS
See Historic Homes: Detillens

MUSEUM OF THE QUEEN'S ROYAL SURREY REGIMENT
Map 2 Ac /p36
Guildford (0483) 222484 ext 9
Clandon Park, West Clandon, Guildford
Open: early April-mid Oct, Tue-Thur, w/end & BH Mons 14.00-18.00
Free (donations gratefully accepted)
See also Historic Homes: Clandon Park

OLD KILN AGRICULTURAL MUSEUM
Map 2 Aa /p50
Frensham (025125) 2300
Reeds Rd, Tilford ½m S
Farnham off A287
Open: early April-late Sep, Wed-Sun & BHs 11.00-18.00; groups by arrangement
Charge: £1 (ch 50p)
See also Gardens: Old Kiln Agricultural Museum
🅿 ♿ ⛩️

ROYAL ARMY ORDNANCE CORPS MUSEUM
Map 1 Bb
Aldershot (0252) 24431 ext 516
Deepcut, Camberley 2m SE town on B3012
Open: all year, Mon-Thur 8.30-12.30 & 13.30-16.30 (Fri 16.00), closed BHs & selected weeks Aug
Free
No dogs
🅿 ♿

ROYAL MILITARY ACADEMY SANDHURST COLLECTION
Map 1 Ba / p13
Bagshot (0276) 63344 ext 489
Royal Military Academy, Sandhurst 1m SW town off A321
Open: by arrangement in writing
Free
No dogs
🅿

STAINES MUSEUM
Map 1 Ac
Staines (81) 61804
The Market Square, Staines
Open: all year, Wed & Fri 14.00-16.00 (Sat 16.30), closed BHs; groups at other times by arrangement
Free
No dogs
🚻 ♿

THE WATERMILL MUSEUM
Map 4 Ac
Edenbridge (0732) 862914
Haxted, 2½m SE Edenbridge
Open: Easter-end Sep, w/ends 11.00-18.00, also summer school holidays Mon-Thur 14.00-18.00
Charge: 40p (ch 20p), reductions for school groups by arrangement
No dogs
Snacks w/ends only
🅿 🚻 🍽

WEYBRIDGE MUSEUM
Map 1 Bc
Weybridge (97) 43573
Church St, Weybridge
Open: all year, w/days 14.00-17.00 , also 10.00-13.00 Sats & school holidays (closed BHs)
Free
Disabled visitors by arrangement
No dogs
🅿 🚻 ♿

WIMBLEDON LAWN TENNIS MUSEUM
Map 3 Ab
(01) 946 6131
All England Tennis Club, Church Rd, Wimbledon SW19
Open: all year, Tues-Sat 11.00-17.00, Sun 14.00-17.00 (during championships open tournament visitors only), telephone in advance
Charge: £1 (ch & OAPs 50p), group (20) reductions by arrangement
Disabled visitors by arrangement
No dogs
🅿 🚻 ♿

WOMEN'S ROYAL ARMY CORPS MUSEUM
Map 2 Ab
Aldershot (0252) 24431 ext 265
Queen Elizabeth Park, Guildford
Open: all year, w/days 9.00-16.00 (closed Good Fri, 25 & 26 Dec & BHs)
Free
No dogs
🅿 🚻 ♿

Nature Reserves

These protected areas allow plants, trees and wildlife to thrive in their natural habitat. Most of the Surrey countryside has been taken up either for farming or for urban development so nature reserves are particularly important for the study of ecology and for conservation of indigenous plants and wildlife. Too many human visitors would destroy the environment and disturb the wildlife so access to many reserves is restricted.

The reserves listed below are accessible to the public but in many of them this is only because they are crossed by public footpaths. Do not leave the footpaths or in any way disturb the environment.

Organisations

ROYAL SOCIETY FOR NATURE CONSERVATION
Lincoln (0522) 752326
The Green, Nettleham, Lincoln LN2 2NR
The Society is a voluntary organisation founded in 1912 seeking to promote the conservation, study and appreciation of nature and the protection of flora and fauna by creating and establishing nature reserves representing typical natural and semi-natural habitats. It acts as the national association of the local Nature Conservation Trusts which are established on a county or regional basis throughout the UK, providing a coordinating centre for these independent Trusts, administering funds and providing practical advice on conservation to public and private bodies. Together with the Trusts it owns or manages 1200 nature reserves and has a membership of over 128,000

SURREY TRUST FOR NATURE CONSERVATION (STNC)
Guildford (0483) 223526
Secretary: Miss G.E.Dougherty
Hatchlands, East Clandon, Guildford

Reserves

BAGMOOR COMMON
Map 2 Ab
Witley, 1m SW Milford off A3
Access via track from car park through Borough Farm and across stream
34 acres of heath and woodland with glade of mixed shrubs and attractive species of butterfly on western fringe
STNC P

BAY POND
Map 4 Ac
Godstone, 2m SE Redhill at junction of A25 & A22
No access to reserve but good viewing from public footpath along southern boundary
17 acres of lake, swamp & farmland; over 100 species of birds recorded, including little & great crested grebe, kingfisher, wagtail & heron
STNC P

BUSBRIDGE LAKES
Map 2 Ab/p53
Godalming (048 68) 21955
1½m SW Godalming off B2130
Open: BHs only (Easter, May, spring & summer), Suns & Mons 11.00-17.30; schools & groups at other times by arrangement
Charge: £1.20 (ch, OAPs 80p)
37 acres of parkland, lakes & nature trails, sanctuary for over 80 species of exotic waterfowl & birds, also flock of Jacobs sheep; roman relics, gothic boathouse, caves & bridges dating from 16th century
Home produce stall
No dogs
P

EPSOM GREAT POND
Map 3 Ba/p41
Epsom Common, ½m SW Epsom off B280
Open: all year, daily
Part of Epsom Common, originally a monastic stewpond restored in 1976 and now a wildlife reserve; birds include coot, moorhen, mallard, little grebe & mandarin duck
See also Country Parks: Epsom Common
P

HACKHURST DOWNS
Map 2 Ac
4m W Dorking
Open: all year, daily
13 acres of chalk grassland on southern slope of North Downs with good views over Tillingbourne valley; variety of orchids & butterflies
SCC NT P

NOWER WOOD
Map 3 Ba
Headley, 1m SE Leatherhead on B2033
81 acres of woodland containing oak, sweet chestnut, Scots pine, larch & yew; noted also for displays of bluebells & spring flowers; badgers, roe deer, 35 species of birds, butterflies & dragonflies; woodland walk (priced leaflet available)
STNC

Orienteering

PERROTTS WOOD
Map 3 Bb
Banstead Wood Estate, ½m S
Banstead on B2219
Part of Banstead Wood Estate
providing breeding ground for a
variety of birds; visitors must
keep to marked trails; 1½m
nature trail (leaflet available from
Banstead Council Information
Centre)
See also Woodland: Banstead
Wood
🅿

STAFFHURST WOOD
See Woodlands: Staffhurst
Wood

STAINES MOOR
Map 1 Ac
½m NW Staines on A30
Acres of marsh and dry
grassland supporting a range of
plants uncommon in SE
England; regular wintering flock
of golden plover
Spellthorne Borough Council

Orienteering is competitive
navigation on foot. With the aid
of a map and compass,
competitors find their way as
accurately and skilfully as
possible between given points.

Courses vary in length from
about 2km for children and
beginners, to over 12km for
experienced adults. There is
usually a variety of courses to
choose from, including a non-
competitive 'Wayfinders' course.
These permanent courses are
designed specifically for the
casual orienteer.

Events are usually held in
woods, forests, on heath and
moorland, whose paths,
streams, hills and valleys,
provide the most diverse
navigation problems.

The only equipment needed
for orienteering is outdoor
clothes, a red biro for copying
the course, a whistle, a
polythene bag to use as a map
case and a compass. The event
entry fee is usually about 50p-
£1 (juniors 25p-50p)

The British Orienteering
Federation is the central body
for orienteering in England. A
full event calendar with
telephone numbers for enquiries
is obtainable from them on
request. All memebers receive a
copy of 'The Orienteer', a bi-
monthly magazine containing a
full fixture list showing B.O.F.
registered events.

After two or three events, if

you decide you like orienteering, it is best to join your local club. A list is given below.

THE BRITISH ORIENTEERING FEDERATION

Matlock (0629) 3661
41 Dale Rd, Matlock, Derbyshire DE4 3LT
Regional Secretary: R. Lott esq
01-788 2775
2 Glendene, 115 Victoria Rd, London SW19 6PR
Membership Secretary: Marjorie Challis
01-641 2573
25 Rosehills Gardens, Sutton, Surrey

Surrey Orienteering Clubs

CROYDON ORIENTEERING CLUB

Gilliam Smith
75 Upper High St, Epsom
KT17 4RA

DARTFORD ORIENTEERING KLUBB

Mrs L. Kelly
Woldingham (905) 3008
Rushmore, Camp Rd, Woldingham

ENDURANCE RUNNERS ORIENTEERING SOCIETY

Mr Tony Lynn
Crowthorne (0344) 778519
7 Wargrove Drive, Owlsmoor, Camberley

GUILDFORD ORIENTEERS

Mr John White
01-651 4876
131 Sorrel Bank, Linton Glade, Forestdale, Croydon

MOLE VALLEY

Mr M. Elliot
01-640 5785
9 Grosvenor Court, London Rd, Morden

SOUTHERN NAVIGATORS

Mr Michael Yeo
Woking (048 62) 64254
27 Orchard Drive, Horsell, Woking

Other Historic Buildings

HOSPITAL OF THE BLESSED TRINITY

Map 2 Ab
Guildford (0483) 62670
Abbot's Hospital, High St, Guildford
Open: all year, Mon, Wed & Sat 14.00-16.00
Free
Hour lecture, tours for accredited schools, colleges & historical societies by arrangement with the Master

OXENFORD GRANGE
Map 2 Ab
Peper Harow, 2½m SE Farnham
on B3001
Not open to public but visible
from road
Remains of a grange of
Waverley Abbey; converted to a
residence in 1536 but
demolished 1775; decorated
window survives; picturesque
group of farm buildings and
large mock medieval barn built
by Pugin 1843 nearby

VILLAGE CAGE & ST PETER'S CROSS
Map 4 Ac /p83
Lingfield, 2½m N East
Grinstead on B2028
Not open to the public but
visible from outside
Dating from 18th century, built
of local stone but original use
unknown, thought to have been
a look-out or a lock-up

WHITEHALL
Map 3 Bb
(01) 643 1236
1 Malden Rd, Cheam, ½m SE
Ewell on A232
Open: April-Sep, Tue-Fri & Sun
14.00-17.30, Sat 10.00-
17.30; Oct-March, Wed, Thur &
Sun 14.00-17.30, Sat 10.00-
17.30; BH 14.00-17.30
(closed 24 Dec, 2 Jan); groups
by arrangement
Charge: 40p (ch 20p)
No dogs
🚃 ♿ ⚓

Picnic Sites

The following sites have been
specially created for picnics and
usually have picnic tables. They
have car parks, are open at all
times and are free unless
otherwise stated.

ABINGER HIGHRIDGE PICNIC PLACE
Map 4 Aa
1½m E Dorking off A25, 1½m
S Brockham on Brockham to
Newdigate Rd
Pleasant woodland setting on
fringe of oak plantation in rolling
Surrey farmland
🅿

ABBOT'S WOOD PICNIC PLACE
Map 2 Aa
3½m S Farnham, 1½m SE
Bucks Horn Oak on Dockenfield
Rd off A325
Grassy area bordered by Norway
spruce and western red cedars
with views over South Downs
and Buster Hill
1¾m forest walk starts here,
leaflet available
Lavatories
See also Woodlands: Alice
Holt Forest
FC 🅿

LODGE INCLOSURE PICNIC PLACE
Map 2 Aa
1 m W of A325, 3m S Farnham
Attractive grassy glades amidst
old oak woods, fine views over
valley of River Wey

1½m arboretum trail starts
here; ¼m trail for the disabled
See also Woodland: Alice Holt
Forest
FC ▣

LODGE POND PICNIC PLACE
Map 2 Ba
3½m S Farnham, 1m N Bucks
Horn Oak, E of A325
Access via forest road from
information centre, extensive
grass picnic area beside pond
Fishing
See also Woodland: Alice Holt
Forest
FC

GOOSE GREEN PICNIC PLACE
Map 2 Ba
3½m S Farnham, 100 yds W
Bucks Horn Oak off A325
Just inside old oak wood
planted 1820 with fine view
over South Downs
1¼m forest walk starts here
passing an area associated with
Romano-British pottery and a
reconstructed pottery kiln
See also Woodlands: Alice
Holt Forest

NEWLANDS CORNER
Map 2 Ac
1½m E Guildford on A25
Well-known viewpoint and
picnic site at 500ft on the North
Downs
Nearby is the haunted silent
pool, where it is said a local
maiden, hounded by King John,
drowned herself
Lavatories
▣ ☕

NORBURY PARK
Map 4 Aa
2m S Leatherhead, ½m W
Mickleham off A24
Interesting wooded chalk slope
with fine beeches and yews,
path running along River Mole
▣

OCKHAM AND WISLEY COMMONS
Map 4 Aa
1½m SE Cobham off A3
southbound carriageway
Large open space with picnic
tables set amongst trees
Lavatories
▣ ♿ ☕

Riding Stables

This list includes stables offering
riding instruction and hacking
(country rides). Most lessons
are in classes or groups but
private tuition is often available.
Hacking is not usually allowed
unaccompanied unless the
ability of the rider is known.
Stables which provide livery or
stud services are not included.
Exact locations of stables are
not given since it is always
advisable to telephone in
advance.

APRIL COTTAGE STABLES
Tadworth (823) 3979
Stuarts Lane, Walton-on-the-Hill
Open: daily (except Mon)
Lesson/Hack: w/days £6
hour, w/ends £9 hour
One of the best hacks in Surrey
16 mounts, adults only

**BLINDLEY HEATH SCHOOL
OF EQUITATION**
Lingfield (0342) 833317
Olden Craig Farm, Tandridge
Lane
Open: daily
Lessons: £4.60 half hour,
private £4.60 hour, groups
lessons
Specialises in teaching
15 mounts

**BROADLANDS RIDING
CENTRE**
Alton (0420) 63382
Medstead, Alton
Open: daily
Lessons: £5 hour (ch £4)
No hacking
10 mounts

**CLOCK TOWER RIDING
SCHOOL**
(073783) 2874
Brighton Rd, Lower Kingswood
Open: daily (except Mon)
Lessons/Hack: £6 hour
16 mounts

**DIAMOND HANDICAPPED
CENTRE**
See Disabled: Diamond
Handicapped Centre

DORKING RIDING SCHOOL
Dorking (0306) 881718
Ranmore Rd, Dorking
Open: daily (except Thur)
Lesson/Hack: £4 hour
Specialises in teaching
18 mounts

DOWNSWAY STABLES
Leatherhead (03723) 77246
Headley Park Farm, Hurst Lane,
Headley
Open: daily
Lessons/Hacking: £6 hour
30 mounts, comprehensive
instruction, covered school,
floodlit outside menage

FARTHING DOWN STABLES
Downland (71) 51609
Drive Rd, Old Coulsdon
Open: daily (except Mon)
Hack: £4 hour
Lessons: £5 hour, private £4
half hour
7 mounts

**GRANGEFIELD RIDING
SCHOOL**
Guildford (0483) 64328
Old Farm Rd, Guildford
Open: daily (except Mon & Tue)
Lesson/Hack: £4.50 (ch £4)
hour
Specialises in hacking, jumping
16 mounts

**GREENWAYS FARM &
STABLES**
Godalming (04868) 4741
Lower Eashing, Godalming
Open: daily (except Fri & Sun
pm)
Hack: £6 (Mon-Thur)
Lessons: £5.50, private £8
Provides basic tuition
14 mounts

HAWLEY EQUITATION CENTRE
Camberley (0276) 31990
Hawley Park, Camberley
Open: daily (except Mon)
Lessons/Hack: £7 w/days, £9
(ch £6) w/ends & evenings
 Specialises hacking, jumping &
flatwork
25 mounts

LITTLE BROOK EQUESTRIANS
Lingfield (0342) 832360
East Park Lane, New Chapel,
Lingfield
Open: daily (except Mon)
Lessons: £5 private hour
Specialises in individual tuition
for competitive riders at all
levels
5 mounts

LOWER FARM RIDING & LIVERY STABLES
Cobham (266) 7545
Lower Farm Stables,Stoke Rd,
Stoke d'Abernon, Cobham
Open: daily
Lessons/Hacks: £4 hour
w/days, £4.50 w/ends
Private bridle way to superb
hacking
35 mounts

OAKS PARK RIDING SCHOOL & LIVERY STABLES
Burgh Heath (07373) 53278
Carshalton Rd, Woodmansterne
Open: daily (except Mon)
Lessons: £5.50 hour
Hacking for experienced riders
only
15 mounts

ORCHARD COTTAGE RIDING STABLES
Reigate (07372) 41311
Babylon Lane, Lower
Kingswood
Open: daily (except Thurs)
Hack: £6.50 hour
Lesson: £6.50 ¾ hour
General teaching, reductions for
housewives & children after
school, also evening rides
12 mounts

ORCHARD POYLE CARRIAGE HIRE
Egham (87) 35983
South Gate Carriage Stables,
Wick Lane, Englefield Green
Open: daily
Lessons: driving £10 hour
Also carriages for hire for special
occasions, weddings & livery
stables

PRIORY SCHOOL OF EQUITATION
Frensham (025125) 3697
Mill Bridge, Frensham
Open: daily
Lessons/Hack: £6 hour
General riding school

SOUTHBOROUGH LODGE FARM
Godalming (048 68) 21408
Shackleford, Godalming
Open: daily
Lessons/Hack: £5 hour, £6 private hour
Riding holidays, disabled riders welcome
9 mounts
&

VALE LODGE STABLES
Leatherhead (03723) 73184
Downs Lane, Leatherhead
Open: daily
Lessons/Hack: £5 hour
Beginners & children
11 mounts

WALTON HEATH LIVERY & TRAINING ESTABLISHMENT
Tadworth (823) 3118
4 Chapel Rd, Tadworth
Open: daily (except Mon), 9.30-17.30
Lesson/Hack: £10-£12 private hour; beginners & new clients £2.50 half hour; other prices vary
Specialises also in side saddle lessons
14 mounts

WILDWOODS RIDING CENTRE
Tadworth (823) 2146
Ebbisham Lane, Walton-on-the-Hill, Tadworth
Open: daily
Lessons/Hack: telephone for details, prices start at £5.50
Advanced & novice riders welcome, evening rides, hacking in beautiful countryside
20 mounts

River Trips

RUNNYMEDE BOATHOUSE
Egham (87) 37020
Windsor (95) 51900
French Bros., Windsor Rd, Old Windsor
Return trips from Runnymede Boathouse to Hampton Court
Departs: mid May-mid Sep, Mon, Tue, Thur 9.15
Charge: £3.90 (return), £2.60 (single)
2 hour return cruise to Windsor or Staines
Departs: Easter-Oct, Wed & Sun 14.14
Charge: £2 (ch £1)
Regular return trips through Runnymede, passing Magna Carta Island and the Memorials (Cooper's Hill)
Departs: Easter-Oct, daily

Charge: 90p (ch 45p)
Reductions for groups, the
disabled and OAPs by
arrangement
Qualified guides available at
additional cost
  ♿ 🛏 ✕ ♀

GUILDFORD BOATHOUSE
Guildford (0483) 504494
Millbrook, Guildford
Departs: Easter-Sep, Tue-Sun
14.00
Charge: £1.50 (ch £1)
1½ hour trip on board the
'Harry Stevens' launch departing
from Guildford and cruising
upstream through St Catherine's
Lock, then turning back at the
entrance to the old Arun Canal
Also available is the 'Alfred
Leroy Cruising Restaurant',

Sailing

ROYAL YACHTING ASSOCIATION
Thames Valley Region
Secretary: C.E. Blamey esq
15 Hyburn Close, St Albans
The Association is the co-
ordinating organisation for the
sport and organises proficiency
schemes. The following clubs
are all members of the Royal
Yachting Association.

ASSOCIATION OF THAMES YACHT CLUBS
Secretary: E.H. Fountain
Warborough (086 732) 8663
4 Plough Close, Shillingford,
Oxon
This association aims to
promote and protect the
interests of private boat owners
on the Thames and to develop
good fellowship between clubs
and members

Sailing Clubs

AQUARIUS SAILING CLUB
Secretary: N.C. Knowles
8 Cranes Park Crescent,
Surbiton

BURGHFIELD SAILING CLUB
Secretary: J. Ridehalgh
22 Stream Farm Close, Lower
Bourne, Farnham

**CHARTERHOUSE SAILING
CLUB**
Secretary: Master I-C Sailing
Charterhouse, Godalming

**FRENSHAM POND SAILING
CLUB**
Secretary: Mrs Sylvia Rhodes
10 Pine Drive, Hawley,
Camberley

**GUILDFORD COASTAL
CRUISING CLUB**
Secretary: Mrs S. Robinson
Langley, Lime Grove, Camberley

**HAWLEY LAKE SAILING
CLUB**
Secretary: Major B. Dyer
R.A.P.C.
3 TRG Regt. R.E., Southwood
Camp, Cove, Farnborough

LALEHAM SAILING CLUB
Secretary: A.A. Turnbull
20 Oakfield Drive, Reigate

**LITTLETON SAILING CLUB
(C.S.S.A.)**
Treasurer: Geoffrey Hunt
39 Hazel Ave., Guildford

LONDON PIRATES
Treasurer: A.H.J. Davis
54 Coombe Lane, West
Kingston-upon-Thames

**LONDON RIVER YACHT
CLUB**
Secretary: H.C. Shields
23 River Court, Portsmouth Rd,
Surbiton

**MERTON YOUTH SAILING
CLUB**
Secretary: T. Baptie
226 London Rd, Mitcham

**MIDDLE THAMES YACHT
CLUB**
Secretary: Joan D. Mawhinney
Worgl, Wentworth Close, Ripley

MINIMA YACHT CLUB
Miss J. Mayes
48A High St., Kingston-upon-
Thames

OFFSHORE CRUISING CLUB
Vice Admiral: Peter Wicher
Widgers Wood, Sheets Heath,
Brookwood, Woking

PAPERCOURT SAILING CLUB
Secretary: J.L. Bartlett
Little Ripley House, High St,
Ripley

PENTON HOOK YACHT CLUB
Secretary: The Clubhouse
Penton Hook Marina, Staines
Lane, Chertsey

ROYAL CANOE CLUB
Secretary: Mrs Barnard
97 Riverbank, Laleham Rd,
Staines

SMALL BOAT CLUB
Secretary: Mrs E.A. Woodger
10 Northcote Ave, Tolworth,
Surbiton

SOUTHWEST SAILING CLUB
Secretary: D. Armitage
2 Fir Rd, Sutton

THAMES MOTOR YACHT CLUB
Secretary; M. Shefras
29 The Ridings, Epsom

THAMES SAILING CLUB
The Secretary: The Clubhouse,
Portsmouth Rd, Surbiton

THAMES VALLEY CRUISING CLUB
Secretary: Mrs B. Currie
7 Forest Hills, Camberley

WALTON-ON-THAMES SAILING CLUB
Secretary: G.J. Potter
2 Meadow Rd, Burpham,
Guildford

WEYBRIDGE MARINERS CLUB
Secretary: J. Creese
21 Fortesque Rd, Weybridge

WEY CRUISING CLUB
Secretary: Mrs Kathleen Gates
2 William Rd, Guildford

Skiing

SANDOWN SKI SCHOOL
Esher (78) 65588
Sandown Park, More Lane,
Esher
Open: Sep-Easter, w/days
19.00-21.00, w/ends selected
times (telephone for details);
March-Aug private lessons &
practice; groups (10-12) by
arrangement
Charge: 6 hour course £26 (ch
£20); Sep, free 2 hours; Oct
free hour (prices include boots,
skis, sticks, instruction & lift)
Beginners and advanced
🅿 🍽️✕

STAINFORTH SKI CENTRE
Aldershot (0252) 25889
Hurst Rd, Aldershot
Open: all year, daily, telephone
for details of lessons, courses
and open practice
Courses: instruction for
beginners, advanced private
lessons, school courses
Charge: 6 hour courses from
£25 (includes equipment)

Sports Centres

These centres offer a wide range of activities. Full timetables and charges are available from each centre. Membership fees given are for a year. Charges given are a selection. Where necessary, changing rooms and showers are provided. Opening times given are for the centres, not for any specific activities. Many of the activities will be organised by clubs. Full details from each centre. Centres often provide detailed brochures.

CRANLEIGH RECREATION CENTRE
Map 2 Bc
Cranleigh (0483) 274400
Village Way, Cranleigh
Open: all year, daily 9.00-21.30
Facilities: squash, swimming', multi-gymn
Charges: swimming 70p (ch 35p), squash £1.30 half hour (off peak 70p), coaching £1.20 half hour, spectators 20p
Courses: swimming, squash, slimming club (Tue), activities for ch during school holidays
🅿 ♿ 🍴

EGHAM SPORTS CENTRE
Map 1 Ac
Lidington (873) 7695
Vicarage Rd, Egham
Open: all year, w/days 7.30-23.00, w/ends 8.00-23.00 (closed 25 & 26 Dec)

Facilities: squash, weight training, sports hall
Courses: various, badminton, squash, trampoline, judo, karate
Charges: squash £2.40 (mornings), £2.25 (off peak), £2.50 (peak); badminton £3 hour; hall £12 hour
🅿 ♿ 🍴 ☕

ELMBRIDGE LEISURE CENTRE
Map 3 Aa
Walton-on-Thames (98) 43863
Sunbury Lane, Walton-on-Thames
Open: all year, daily 9.00-23.00 (closed Good Fri, 25 & 26 Dec, 1 Jan)
Facilities: squash, badminton, trampoline, yoga (bookings for winter courses taken Sep)
Membership: 30p day membership, £9.50 annual membership, £17 family (ch16-17 £5.50, ch5-15 £3.50, OAPs £2.50)
Charges: squash £2.80 hour, badminton £2.50 hour, Gymn 90p session
🅿 🚊 ♿ 🍴 ☕

FARNHAM SPORTS CENTRE
Map 2 Aa
(0252) 723208
Farnham, Dogflud Way
Open; telephone for details
Facilities: archery, badminton, basketball, 5-a-side football, gymnastics, judo, keep-fit, squash, swimming, table tennis, trampoline
Courses: details and application forms from reception

Charges: squash £1.30 half hour (70p off peak), badminton £2.40 hour (ch 75p), £1.65 off peak (ch 75p), ladies' recreation £1 session; sports hall £15 hour (£7.50 off peak), half hall £7.50 hour (£3.75 off peak) Telephone bookings w/days 9.00-22.00, Sun 9.00-18.00, 48 hours notice for cancellation ☂ ⌂ ♀

GUILDFORD SPORTS CENTRE
Map 2 Ab
Guildford (0483) 571651
Bedford Rd, Guildford
Open: all year, Mon, Thur & Fri 12.00-19.00, Weds 12.00-20.00, Tue 13.00-20.00, w/ends 9.00-17.00
Facilities: swimming pool, squash, weight training, keep-fit, table tennis, badminton, trampoline, cricket, archery
Courses: swimming, judo, karate, Martial Arts during school holidays
Charge: swimming 75p (30p), off peak 45p; squash £1.60 hour; keep-fit 85p per session
P ☂ ⌂ ♀

HASLEMERE SPORTS CENTRE
Map 2 Bb
Haslemere (0428) 2124
Lime Green, Shottermill, Haslemere
Open: all year, Tue & Wed 6.15-19.40, Thur 6.15-18.40, Fri 6.15-17.40, w/ends 9.00-16.40
Facilities: swimming, squash, tennis, netball
Courses: swimming, squash, tennis

Charges: swimming 56p (ch & OAPs 28p); squash £1.50 40 mins; tennis £1.50 hour; netball £4 hour
P ☂ ⌂

LEATHERHEAD LEISURE CENTRE
Map 3 Ba
Leatherhead (0372) 377674
Guildford Rd, Leatherhead
Open: all year, w/days 9.30-22.30, w/ends 9.30-20.00, BHs 9.00-17.30
Facilities: various including, squash, badminton, table tennis, keep-fit, tennis, roller skating, swimming
Courses: various, swimming, yoga, aerobics, badminton, self defence, fitness training
Charges: squash £1.10 half hour (60p off peak), fitness session £1.10, tennis court £1.50 hour
Membership: £1 joining fee; family £16.50 (ch16); adult £10; junior, OAP & disabled £4.50
Telephone bookings by members 7 days in advance, non-members 6 days in advance in person after 9.30, cancellation fee
P ☂ ⌂ ♀

STAINES YOUTH SPORTS CENTRE
Map 1 Ac
Staines (81) 53220
Leacroft, Staines
Open: telephone for details, programme available from above address or Staines Library
Facilities: sports hall, badminton, keep-fit, 5-a-side football

Membership: £5 (under 18s £2.50), subscription fee 35p (25p)
Charges: courts £3 hour (non members), 3 courts £10 hour; telephone for details
Courses: table tennis, badminton, archery
🅿 ☕

WOKING LEISURE CENTRE
Map 1 Bc
Woking (048 62) 71789
Woking Park, Woking
Open: all year, w/days 9.30-22.00, Sat 9.00-21.00 & Sun 9.00-17.00
Facilities: various, including squash, badminton, cricket nets, archery, gym, judo, keep-fit, weight training, projectile room, all weather outdoor pitch
Courses: varous
Charges: squash £1.50 half hour (£1 off peak), badminton £1.90 half hour (£1.30 off peak), keep-fit 50p
🅿 ♿ ☕

YEOMANS BRIDGE SPORTS CENTRE
Map 2 Aa
Aldershot (0252) 25484
Manor Rd, Ash, Near Aldershot
Open: school term, Mon, Wed & Fri 17.00-22.00, Tue & Thur 18.00-22.00, w/ends 9.00-22.00; school holidays, w/days 13.00-22.00, w/ends 9.00-22.00
Facilities: sports hall, table tennis, badminton, gym, outside tennis courts
Charges: badminton £2.60 hour, sports hall £8.50 hour, outdoor pitch £2.50 hour (flood lit £4.50), tennis £1-£2.10
🅿 ♿ ☕

Swimming Pools

Banstead

BANSTEAD SWIMMING POOL
Merlin Rise, Banstead
Main pool 25m

Cranleigh

CRANLEIGH RECREATION CENTRE
Cranleigh (048 66) 4400
Main pool 25m; learner pool 12.57 x 7.31ml; room for 120 spectators

Dorking

DORKING SWIMMING CENTRE
Dorking (0306) 87722
Reigate Rd, Dorking
Main pool 25m x 10m; learner pool 9m x 6.5m; room for 30 spectators

Epsom

MUNICIPAL BATHS
Epsom (78) 22111
Main pool 30m; diving facilities, spring board 1m, fixed 1m, 3m & 5m; room for 412 spectators

Swimming

Farnham

FARNHAM SPORTS CENTRE
Farnham (0252) 723208
Main pool 25m

Godalming

BROADWATER PARK
Godalming (048 68) 7282
Godalming
Main pool 25m

Guildford

GUILDFORD SPORTS CENTRE
Guildford (0483) 71651
Bedford Rd, Guildford
Main pool 33.3m x 12.5m,
depth 1-2m; learner pool
12.5m x 7.5m, depth 1m;
diving pool 12m x 11m, depth
3.85m, boards at 1m, 3m &
5m; room for 170 spectators

Haslemere
SWIMMING POOL
Haslemere (0428) 2124
Lime Green, Shottermill,
Haslemere
Main pool 25m, 6 lanes;
paddling pool
See also Sports Centres:
Haslemere Sports Centre

Horley

HORLEY SWIMMING POOL
Horley (029 34) 4075
Thornton Close, Horley
Main pool 25m; room for 50
spectators

Leatherhead

LEATHERHEAD LEISURE CENTRE
Leatherhead (53) 77676
Guildford Rd, Leatherhead
Main pool 25m x 12.5m, depth
1-2m; diving pool 1m x 1.8,
depth 3-4m, boards at 1m &
3m; learner pool 12.5m x
7.5m, depth 600-900mm with
steps; room for 20 spectators

Reigate

REIGATE BATHS
Reigate (74) 43145
Castlefield Rd, Reigate
Main pool 22m

Staines

STAINES SWIMMING POOL
Staines (81) 53171
Knowle Green, Staines
Main pool 33.1 x 3m; learner
pool; diving facilities

Walton

WALTON SWIMMING POOL
Walton (98) 22984

Woking

WOKING BATHS
Woking (048 62) 68825
Clarence Ave, Woking
Main pool 25m

Tennis

Lawn Tennis

Surrey has over 146 tennis
clubs affiliated to the Lawn
Tennis Association, the
governing body for the sport in
this country. In addition there
are hundreds of public tennis
courts and information on these
can be obtained from local
council offices.

For any information on the
sport and for details of local
clubs, too numerous to mention
here in full, contact:

**LAWN TENNIS
ASSOCIATION**
(01) 385 2366
Barons Court, West Kensington,
London W14 9EG

**SURREY COUNTY LAWN
TENNIS ASSOCIATION**
Secretary: J C Robbins Esq
52 Fairfax Ave, Epsom KT17
2QP

Real Tennis

'Real Tennis' or 'Royal Tennis' is
known in Austria and France
under its ancient name 'jeu de
paume'. It is one of the oldest
ball games in existence played
by 2 or 4 players with a hard
ball and rackets of various
shapes and sizes.

The royal tennis court at
Hampton Court (**See Historic
Homes**), built in 1529 by
Henry VIII, is the oldest court
where the game is still played.

A book of rules and a concise
history of real tennis is available
from the Committee of the
Royal Court, Palace Bookshop,
Hampton Court Palace
(telephone 01-977 8441)

**ROYAL COURT
Map 3 Aa**
(01) 977 3015
Hampton Court Palace,
Hampton Court
Open: April-end Sep, daily
9.30-17.45
Charge: non-members £2.40
(under 23s £1.50), telephone in
advance
Hire: racquet 50p, coaching
£3.80-£6.50 by arrangement
only
Professional: Chris Ronaldson,
the current World Champion
The fixture secretary will supply
details of national and club
matches

Tourist Information Offices

Tourist Information Offices can be helpful whether you are a visitor to Surrey or a resident. They have a wealth of information on local attractions, places to stay and eat, events, activities, history and much more. For example if you have trouble in contacting any of the places listed in this directory contact the local information office for help. If you want to find out what you can do in your area contact your local information office and always make a point of contacting the information office at any place you are intending to visit.

SOUTH EAST REGIONAL TOURIST OFFICE
Tunbridge Wells (0892) 40766
Cheviot House, Tunbridge Wells
TN1 1NH
This is the co-ordinating office for all tourist information in the South East of England and it covers Surrey, Kent, East & West Sussex

FARNHAM
Godalming (048 68) 4104 ext 554
Locality Office, South Street

GATWICK
Crawley (0293) 502042
South East England Tourist Board Arrivals Concourse
2nd Floor, Terminal Building, Gatwick, West Sussex

GUILDFORD
Guildford (0483) 67314
Civic Hall, London Rd, Guildford

WALTON-ON-THAMES
Walton-on-Thames (09322) 28844
Town Hall, New Zealand Ave

WOKING
Woking (04862) 5931 ext 319
Council Offices
Guildford Road

Unusual Outing

THORPE PARK
Map 1 Ac
Chertsey (09328) 62633
Staines Lane, Chertsey
400 acres of parkland and lakes form Britain's first 'Theme park' focusing on 'The achievement of British people as a maritime nation'. The exhibits include: New Treasure Island, Model World, aircraft & seaplanes, water gardens, bird sanctuary, nature trail, land-trains and waterbuses for transport around the park, phantome fantasia, cinema 180, roller rink, boats for hire, live entertainment.

Available at additional cost are water sport instruction, water skiing, board sailing, jet skis, trout fishing.
Open: March-July, daily 10.00-18.00; July-Sep, daily 10.00-21.00
Charge: £3.50 (ch & OAPs £2.50), groups £3 (ch & OAPs £2)
Discounts for educational and handicapped groups Mon-Sat only (not BHs) by arrangement
🅿 🥾 ♿ ⬛🍴

Vineyard

HASCOMBE VINEYARDS LTD
Map 2 Bb
(048 632) 343
Hascombe, 1 m SE Godalming on B2130
Open: all year by arrangement only (telephone for details)
Charge: £2.50
8 acre vineyard with modern equipment
Tours, wine tasting & wine shop
🅿 🥾

Walking

Although much of Surrey has been swallowed by suburban London, there remains some beautiful countryside of sandy commonland and heath, offering ideal conditions for walking. The rural areas, mainly south of the Downs and most of the county, are now protected from further urban encroachment. They are easily accessible by hundreds of footpaths and trails, including the ancient long-distance pathway, the North Downs Way which reaches its highest point at Leith Hill and provides breathtaking panoramic views of the surrounding countryside. Whether you are interested in short strolls through parkland, walking in open countryside or following public footpaths through cultivated hills and valleys, the choices are endless.

For the serious walker there are many long walks, but those interested in a short stroll are also well catered for. To begin this section here are some suggestions for shorter walks along marked trails and walks set out in leaflets. Details can be found in other sections of the Leisure A-Z.

MARKED TRAILS
Many organisations have marked walks and produce leaflets to accompany walks which explain the landscape and describe the plant and wildlife encountred. These walks are often through Forestry Commission woodland, country

Walking

parks, nature reserves, locations offering fine views and areas of outstanding beauty. Many start from car parks, picnic sites and nature reserves. A useful publication is 'Discovering Walks in Surrey' by Angela Haine and Susan Owen, both experienced Surrey walkers who have set out eighteen circular walks of varying length with accompanying maps.

The Mole Valley District Council produce a series of leaflets describing a range of varied walks, selected to include a variety of features from panoramic views to historical buildings and aspects of the countryside:
Mole Valley District Council Leatherhead (0372) 374411
Red House, Leatherhead

Organisations

RAMBLERS' ASSOCIATION
Southern Area
1-5 Wandsworth Rd, London SW8 2LJ
The Ramblers' Association campaigns for public access to all rural areas. Its members keep paths clear and fight any development which hinders access to public footpaths. They also waymark paths to make them easier to follow and work to protect the landscape.

The RA also organises excursions and group walks, including trips to different areas of the country. There are hundreds of RA groups throughout Britain, keeping a close watch on footpaths and ensuring they are well maintained, as well as enjoying walking together. Even those who prefer to walk alone may consider joining the RA since it is responsible for enabling the lone walkers to have unhindered access to the countryside.

If you come across a public footpath which is closed, is not accessible or is in any way impassable you should contact the Surrey RA (see below) and report this.

The RA also publishes many leaflets on all aspects of its work as well as a Bed & Breakfast Guide for walkers and a regular journal (free to members).
Membership: £6; couple £7.50; couple retired £3.75; ch 18, students, unemployed & OAP £3; life membership £240, members get free copy Bed & Breakfast Guide (each year), free journal 'Rucksack' (3 each year), local area news, access to Ordnance Survey 1:50,000 map library; special offers & reductions on publications and from shops

SURREY RAMBLERS ASSOCIATION
Secretary: Jim Spencer
Bookham (31) 58571
18 Richmond Way
Fetcham
Please enclose s.a.e. if your require a reply

Long Distance Pathways

GREENSAND WAY
Route: 50m from Haslemere, following Greensand Ridge via Thursley, Hascombe, Pitch Hill, Leith Hill, Bletchingly, Limpsfield and on to Folkestone and Eastbourne in Kent. The Highest point is Leith Hill.
 Suggested access points:
Pitch Hill & Tandridge
For further information contact: Surrey Amenity Council, 2 Jenner Road, Guildford

NORTH DOWNS WAY
Route: runs across Surrey for 40 miles from Farnham to Tatsfield via Guildford, Newlands Corner, Dorking and Godstone, then through Kent to Canterbury or Dover, 150 miles in all. Officially opened in 1978 the North Downs Way follows the crest of the North Downs wherever possible and coincides in places with the ancient Pilgrim's Way. The route is waymarked with the Countryside Commission's official 'acorn' sign.
 Suggested access points:
Chilworth and Ranmore Common
Surrey County Council produces a leaflet which describes the public open spaces, town or villages and facilities to be found in the vicinity of the North Downs Way in Surrey:
Surrey County Council, County Hall, Kingston-upon-Thames

THE WEY-SOUTH PATH
36 miles walking route following the Wey and Arun course from Guildford through into Sussex.

THE DOWNS LINK
Bridleway linking the North and South Downs

Walking Groups

CROYDON & DISTRICT R.A.
Secretary: Mrs J. Spayne
18 Almonday, Mitcham

EAST SURREY R.A.
Secretary: Mr E.A.L. Frost
35 Ingleboro Drive, Purley

FARNHAM & DISTRICT
Secretary: Mrs D. Giles
16 The Chine, Wrecclesham, Farnham

GODALMING & HASLEMERE R.A.
Secretary: Mr M.J. Stubbs
Rylands, Gasden Lane, Witley, Godalming

KINGSTON & DISTRICT R.A.
Secretary: Miss M.P. Goulding
23 Elton Close, Hampton Wick, Kingston

MOLE VALLEY R.A.
Secretary: Mr J. Spencer
18 Richmond Way, Fetcham, Leatherhead

RICHMOND R.A.
Secretary: Mrs B.V. Thomas
50 Breamwater Gardens, Ham, Richmond

Water Skiing

Water skiing is best undertaken as a member of a recognised club. The British Waterski Federation (BWF) is the governing body for sport in Britain and most clubs are affiliated to it, including all those listed below.

If you wish to learn how to water ski contact a club near you. Clubs with vacancies may be able to provide equipment and instruction. The BWF run many courses and should be contacted for details.

Most clubs will hire equipment such as wet suits and usually provide boats. In many cases members are not allowed to use their own boats since the number of boats operating in any one area of water must be carefully controlled.

For any information on the sport contact:

BRITISH WATER SKI FEDERATION
Secretary: Gillian Hill
(01) 387 9371 Upper Woburn Place, London WC1H OQL

DISABLED WATER SKI ASSOCIATION
See Disabled: Water Skiing

Water Ski Clubs

HAWLEY WATER SKI CLUB
Yateley (0252) 876622
Hawley Hard, Gibraltar Barracks, Camberley
Secretary: Mr Neville Eyre
Alton (0420) 86615
36 Tilney Close, Alton, Hampshire
Membership: £17
Facilities for slalom

THORPE PARK
Public Ski School, Chertsey
Charge: £7.90 15 min session, includes instruction, wetsuits & equipment; table ski tow 2 half mile circuits £1; jet skis £5 15 mins, £8 half hour
See also Unusual Outings: Thorpe Park

VARNE BOAT CLUB
New Romney (06793) 2993
The Greens, Coast Drive, Littlestone
Secretary: Mr Brian Newland, 6a Strathmore Close, Caterham
Membership: £40
Facilities for boat owning members and casual skiers

WIREMILL WATER SKI CLUB
Wiremill Lane, New Chapel, Lingfield
Secretary: R Stephens, 51 Banstead Rd, Caterham
Membership: £120 plus £20 joining fee
Facilities for jump & slalom

Windsurfing

If you are a capable windsurfer and have your own sail board you can use it on the inland waters of Surrey, though they are mostly controlled and only private clubs have access to them for sports such as windsurfing. This section gives details of these clubs (many of which have exclusive access to inland waters) and of courses for learning windsurfing. Some of the clubs are sailing clubs with windsurfing members. Other clubs are purely for windsurfing. Some clubs, particularly the sailing clubs, offer a wide range of facilities from bars and restaurants to dressing rooms and showers. It is usually necessary to wear a wetsuit when windsurfing in this country and they can often be hired, as can the sailboards.

LONGSIDE LAKE WINDSURFING SCHOOL
Opposite Thorpe Park, Chertsey
Courses: April-Oct, daily 10.00-19.00; elementary 2 day course (or 4 evenings), 7-8 hours £33
Sea courses from lake for advanced boardsailers
Changing facilities
🅿 ⛲

THORPE PARK
Staines Lane, Chertsey
Public board sailing school
Courses: beginnners only 6 hours £27.50;
novice/finisher course for those with some experience £17 half day (3 hours);
advanced (tuition in freestyle) £5 hour; all courses except advances include equipment, wetsuits and admission to park
Board hire: £5 hour, 2 hours £8, 3 hours £10, £3 every additional hour
Charge: (with own board) £4 hour, 2 hours £5, 3 hours £6, every additional hour £2 (prices include admission to park & use of facilities)
Advisable to book courses 7 days in advance
See also Water Skiing: Thorpe Park
🅿 ⛲ 🛋 ✕ 🍸

WILLOW PARK BOARDSAILING CLUB
Woking (048 62) 23757
Youngs Drive, Ash
Courses: all year, daily w/days £25, w/ends £30 (2½ days of 2 × 4 hours)
RYA approved
Board hire, storage facilities, board sales, shower, changing rooms

WHITEWATER SPORTS WINDSURFING SCHOOL
Silvermere Country Club, Silvermere Lake, Walton-on-Thames
Courses: daily, elementary 10.00-17.00 £27 (includes equipment, insurance & rescue boat)
RYA approved
Changing rooms, showers
P 🍴

Women's Institute

The Women's Institute is a completely independent voluntary organisation, with a total membership of about 400,000 women in England, Wales, the Channel Islands and the Isle of Man.

The broad purpose of the WI is to give countrywomen the opportunity of working together to improve the quality of life in rural areas; and to provide a wide variety of educational and leisure activities. New members are always welcome. WIs usually meet once a month in a hall, parish room or perhaps a school.

If you want to find out more about the WI in your area contact the NFWI local secretary in Surrey.

THE NATIONAL FEDERATION OF WOMEN'S INSTITUTES
Membership Secretary
01-730 7212
39 Eccleston Street
London SW1W 9NT

SURREY FEDERATION OF WOMEN'S INSTITUTES
Secretary: Mrs Freeman
Guildford (0483) 62523
2 Denmark, Guildford

Woodland

This section includes forests, woods, arboretums. Many of them are owned and managed by the Forestry Commission (FC). Woodlands mentioned are open at all times and access is free unless otherwise stated.

ABINGER MOUNTAIN WOOD
Map 2 Ac
1m SW East Horsley off A246
Mainly coniferous woodland including pine, Douglas fir, beech and birch with dense rhododendron thicket
3m and 1m forest walks start ½m E East Horsley at the Surrey County Council car park at Greendene
P

ABINGER EAST HORSLEY FOREST
Map 2 Ac
2m SW East Horsley of A246,
E of Mountain Wood
Woodlands of the former
Lovelace Estate with examples
of ornamental flint, red brick
stonework; bridges including
Dorking Arch and Briary
Bridges; fine views north from
Dorking Arch
5m and 4m forest walks start
from Abinger Mountain Wood
walk
FC ▣

ABINGER RANMORE FOREST
Map 4 Aa
2½m W Dorking on Dorking to
East Horsley by-road of A25
Woodlands on the lip of North
Downs escarpment with views
south to Dorking and Leith Hill,
also east over the Weald; 1 m
forest walk starts at NT car
park
FC ▣

ALICE HOLT FOREST
Map 2 Aa
2m S Farnham on A325
Historic forest, formerly royal
hunting forest with associations
dating from Roman times
Information Centre, ½m forest
walk through oak, pine and
beech woods
See also Picnic Sites: Goose
Green Picnic Place
FC ▣ ♿

BANSTEAD WOOD ESTATE
Map 3 Bb
½m SE Banstead on B2219
300 acres of woodland with
variety of trees including silver
birch, Douglas fir, hazel, wild
cherry, horse chestnut and
rhododendrons
Lavatories
See also Nature Reserves:
Perrot's Wood
▣ ⌣

MOUNTAIN WOOD
Map 2 Ac
2½m E Guildford on A246
Coniferous wood of pine,
Douglas fir, beech & birch
3m walk starts at County
Council car park, Greendene,
also 1m rhododendron walk
FC ▣

NOWER WOOD
See Nature Reserves: Nower
Wood

STAFFHURST WOOD
Map 4 Ac
½m S Limpsfield on Limpsfield
to Haxted road off A25
93 acres of ancient oak
woodlands, 2m nature trail
Surrey County Council

THE TITSEY PLANTATION
Map 3 Bc
Lewes (079 16) 5411
½m N Limpsfield on B269
Open: Easter-end Oct. daily
10.00-16.00
Free
Woodland of mixed deciduous
and coniferous trees within the
4,00 acre Titsey Estate (Titsey
Place & grounds not open to
public)
4½m woodland walk (leaflet
available), superb views of the
Weald
Owned by the Titsey Foundation
P ☐🎋

WITLEY COMMON
See Country Parks: Witley
Common

WITLEY HOLMEN'S GROVE
Map 2 Bb
2m N Haslemere on A286
Forestry Commission plantation
of young conifers, 1m forest
walk
Horseriding by permit only
(apply Alice Holt information
centre)
FC **P**

Zoos

BIRDWORLD
Map 2 Aa
Bentley (0420) 22140
Holt Pound, 3m SW Farnham
on A325
Open: all year, daily 9.30-18.00
(closed 25 Dec)
Charge: £1.30 (ch 85p) bird
garden; 45p (ch 35p) aquarium;
group reductions
Zoological bird gardens &
aquarium
No dogs
P 🍴♿☐

CHESSINGTON ZOOLOGI-CAL GARDENS
Map 3 Ba
Epsom (78) 27227
½m SW Chessington, 3m SE
Esher off A243
Open: all year, daily 10.00-
17.00 (closed 25 Dec)
Charge: Winter, £2.25 (ch
£1.20), Summer £3.25 (ch £1.85),
family and group reductions
Large collection of animals &
birds in 65 acres of countryside;
fun-fair & model railway during
summer months
No dogs
P 🍴♿☐🎋

Acknowledgements

The author and publishers
would like to thank the many
organisations and individuals
for their help and co-operation
in providing information for this
book.